S0-AVE-230

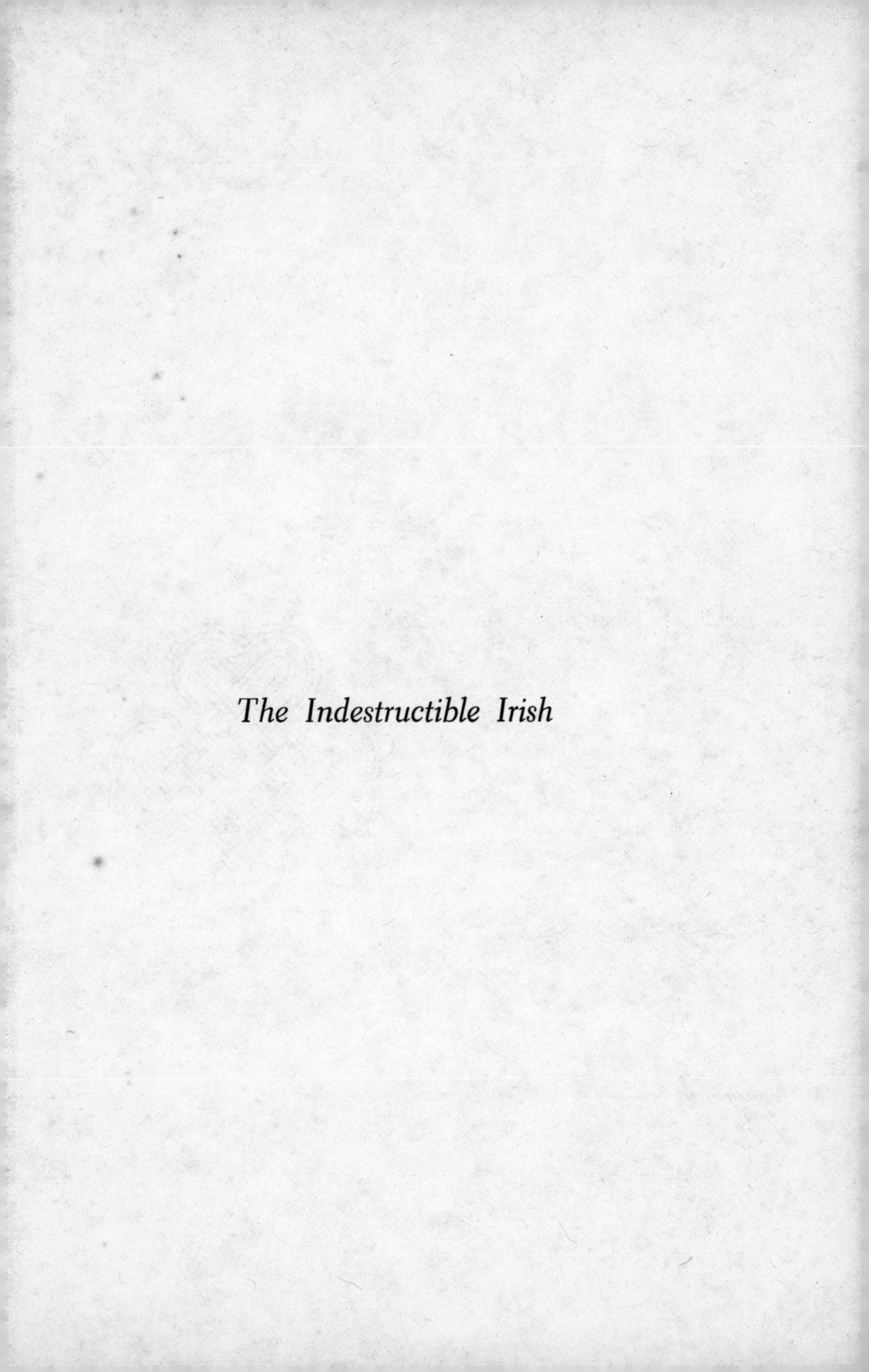

*The Indestructible Irish*

# The Indestructible Irish

John Philip Cohane

*Meredith Press* NEW YORK

*To*

DEIRDRE

ALEXANDER

*and*

CANDIDA

*and to*

THADY WYNDHAM-QUIN,

the gallant young Earl of Dunraven, who although a polio victim for many years, has proved himself indestructible in the truest sense of the word.

Copyright © 1969 by John Philip Cohane

All rights reserved. No part of this book in excess of five hundred words may be reproduced in any form without permission in writing from the publisher.

First edition

Designed by Tony Pollicino
Library of Congress Catalog Card Number: 69-19049
Manufactured in the United States of America for Meredith Press

*Unhappy is the man or nation whose destiny depends on the will of another.*

—Theobald Wolfe Tone

I must confess at the beginning that, in spite of being 100 percent Irish by blood, I have never found the Irish, as a race, endearing. Oscar Wilde, every milligram an Irishman in spite of being 100 percent English by blood, observed on quitting Dublin that it was bad enough to live with your own faults without seeing them reflected in those around you. This form of escapism—not so much from myself but from my mirrored selves—was in large part responsible for my divorce from the Irish-Americans of New England as soon as I had reached a state of mobility. The same bigotry, bias, and discrimination which caused Joseph Kennedy, the late President's father, to flee Boston in the twenties, asking an unanswering Establishment the plaintive question, "How long does it take an Irish-American to become an American?" added to the speed of my flight. It was hardly a source of self-congratulation to be Irish in New England forty years ago.

During the period that followed, first at Yale University, later in New York City, I rarely cast my thoughts back on my origin. Like countless young men and women whose parents or grandparents had been born in Europe, I was determined to become an integral part of the brave new world whose limitless horizons stretched out around me. It was only when a certain amount of affluence had come my way and I could stop worrying a bit about the day-to-day situation, when I was on the threshold of middle age and my surroundings looked less new and brave than I had imagined them, that my thoughts turned more and more toward Ireland. Like most of the Irish in America—like most of the native Irish—my ignorance about the small, ocean-encircled island where for some three thousand years the procession of my ancestors had filed into this world, had lived, aged, and died, was abysmal. I approached the subject tentatively by way of the printed page. Then for the first time I visited Ireland. I came for ten days and have stayed ten years.

There has been a splendid, unexpected compensation in what I have done, in having cast myself back into the heartland of these fellow Irishmen whom I still find en masse not the least bit endearing. If I had chosen Bulgaria or Cambodia or Ethiopia, I could not have picked a country with a history so fascinating and packed with drama, so reflected in the present. Nor could I have chosen a race of people who, as individuals, are more provocative, original, unpredictable, and who have resisted more firmly the process of standardization, of sameness, which is slowly spreading across the face of the earth.

This has nothing to do with my being Irish. It has

been an objective rather than a subjective compensation. At times I feel I have landed not on "the rock from which I sprang" but on Mars or Venus. To those Americans who in their travels, like most Americans, are searching for "foreign" countries, let me offer this advice—don't miss Ireland. Just under the surface, and in the hearts and minds of the people, you will discover the most "foreign" country in Europe.

There have been some rude shocks. Frustrations. Bitter as well as sweet surprises. Some mornings I wake up and feel I can't stay another day. Often I think it would be much better if I had never come, or that I would enjoy life far more in Ireland if I didn't have a drop of Irish blood in my veins. When I do go away, which is frequently, it is with a sense of relief. And yet before long I am dying to get back, and when I step off the plane at Shannon or Dublin, occasionally at Cork, it is with a feeling of inexplicable joy, of returning to the only country which is truly part of my flesh and bones and spirit. It is this very identity which causes most of the trouble.

Living in Ireland is like being with a deeply loved parent who is suffering from a lingering disease. It is hard to admire the color of the eyes or the infectious laughter of someone you suspect is mortally ill.

Most visitors to Ireland arrive, admire, and depart in a mild state of shock brought on by surface first impressions—all unaware of what is really going on in a fundamentally unhappy country.

First of all, having seen the Irish in America and in England, bursting out of ancient straitjackets, self-imposed and otherwise, attaining economic, social, and cultural goals undreamed of fifty years ago, it is extremely painful to find them in their own country, after half a century of freedom, still badly educated, still badly housed, with a standard of living as poor as anywhere in Europe, and a seeming incapacity to lift themselves out of the squalor of the past. "Things have improved," protest those who have been here all their lives, and perhaps things have edged up a bit for some. But what can one make of a country with the lowest population per square mile in Europe—which each year loses as many people through death and migration as are born? The figure has stayed, with minor fluctuations, exactly where it was in 1922—about four million, North and South, compared to nearly nine million a century and a half ago.

Or how can one drive through depressing village after depressing village, one-street strings of dilapidated cottages leaning against each other, some decayed and abandoned, interposed with gloomy, faceless pubs, devoid of tree-lined plazas and recreation centers, clusters of new council houses on the outskirts as colorless, and less imaginative, in design as the older dwellings—how can one pass through such graceless centers of life without worrying about what sort of apathy stultifies the native Irish?

Recently Dan Breen, one of the towering heroes of the fight for liberation from the English, stated in a television interview that he was afraid freedom had come too late, that it should have been won in 1798. Ruefully he voiced the opinion that perhaps the years of the Great Hunger, the desperate years of the 1840's, had sapped the vital spirit of the Irish people. Yet in thousands of instances it has been the brothers and sisters, the cousins and children of these very same people who have accomplished so much in other countries, who have created what amounts to a twentieth-century Celtic revolution outside the boundaries of Ireland.

What can one make of the extraordinary fact that, after the same half century of running their own destinies, the Irish still have sitting on their backs throughout the Republic—at least outside Dublin—about 5 percent of the population, who are Anglo-Irish Protestants, almost totally British by blood, alien in traditions, loyalties, and interests, yet dominant socially and economically? There is no native upper or even middle class in the villages or rural areas coming into being to blend with or infuse new blood into this tired vestigial remnant of the former ruling or colonial class in Ireland.

Or how can one relax and enjoy life in the southern part of the country knowing all the time that north of the Border, in the Six Counties which are still part of the United Kingdom, somewhere between 600,000 and 700,000 Irish Roman Catholics are still treated as second- and third-class citizens on their own soil, discriminated against because of their religion, in terms of housing, job opportunities, cultural, political, and civic roles?

Most disheartening of all is the slow realization that the seeming incapacity of the native Irish to cope successfully with the problems of this world stems primarily not from the enervating climate as some claim; not from the highest carbohydrate diet in Europe—a daily fare based on bread, milk, and potatoes—as has been recently suggested; not from the crippling effects of the past as others claim; but from an ingrained, deep-rooted religious training, medieval in essence, which teaches the Irish as soon as they start to walk and talk to believe that the problems of this world are really not worth coping with, that their primary objective is to prepare themselves against the hour when they must face the threat of hell and eternal damnation before the judgment seat of Almighty God.

This was true of the Irish-Americans in New England. It is truer of the Irish in Ireland. Most of them walk in perpetual fear of the afterlife, regard any overt natural manifestations of their bodies with shame and alarm. Hardly the frame of mind in which to tackle the challenge of reshaping a nation after long oppression. From those in high places who have abdicated to the hierarchy most of their responsibilities, down to the twenty-three-acre farmer who strolls outside his door on a misty morning, takes a look at his weed-infested fields, and then goes back to bed again, it is this preoccupation with the next world which helps cast a perpetual blight over the living world of the Irish.

Not that there are no signs of change. Ideas from outside are beginning to penetrate the Irish cocoon. There is more traffic in and out of the country. Young people going abroad are returning with fresh viewpoints (although many who could help the most are staying away forever).

There is simply too much going on outside Ireland today to keep all of it outside. The barriers of traditional censorship are breaking down in a gradual, if not spectacular, fashion. Television—local and, in the eastern half of the country, British—is casting a questioning light into a number of hitherto murky corners, is helping to create a faintly recognizable facsimile of intellectual curiosity.

But only a mild stirring is taking place, scarcely a revolution or a renaissance. And many view even these mild stirrings with dismay, are girding up their gaiters for a last-ditch fight to maintain at all costs the status quo. As of this moment it would appear that the enemies of change will win the battle hands down.

What is most baffling to those who stay in Ireland long enough to dive below the legendary tranquil surface is how the Irish ever got themselves into such a unique predicament. And it is unique. A race of people who in ancient times rose to intellectual and cultural heights unsurpassed in Western Europe, who in other parts of the world have helped and are still helping to accomplish miracles, are sunk in a morass of inadequacy at home.

After generations of protesting loudly against others running their affairs, thanks to the supreme efforts of a tiny handful whose ideals, principles, and objectives were never fully understood by their fellow countrymen, the Irish in the twenty-six counties have had freedom and self-rule thrust upon them. Having been handed control of their own destinies, they seem unable or unwilling to make any massive effort to better themselves. It is almost as though they had decided the conditions they were screaming about fifty years ago were, after all, just about perfect. The contrast with another new nation of ancient people, Israel, is worth brooding over. In Ireland, those who try to improve conditions are usually stopped dead in their tracks before they even get started.

Recently a prominent, truly enlightened but constantly thwarted member of the government made in public the unqualified statement that unless Ireland entered the Common Market "a future as bleak and unprepossessing as the present" lay ahead of the young Irish. Not one person contradicted him that *both* present and future *are* bleak and unprepossessing. Not a single voice of dissent was raised. And yet, if there were a national referendum on the question, the majority of the Irish people—especially when the forces of reaction swung into high gear with the old familiar platitudes—would vote against the Common Market purely because it represented change.

"Better the divil we know, lads," observes Tim, and Mick bobs his head in approval while Rory behind the bar, open-mouthed with admiration at Tim's sagacity, pours them each another Guinness.

My advice to those who are about to visit Ireland is *not* to do what I have done. Don't start worrying about the Irish and the predicament they're in. Enjoy Ireland. Drift in and out of the pubs, plunging into the finest extemporaneous conversations to be found anywhere in the world. Enjoy the endless variety of sports—horse and dog racing, golf (there are over two hundred clubs North and South with miniscule greens fees), shooting, fox hunting, fishing.

Seek out the bustling country fairs, at least one every week somewhere in Ireland. Plan your visit to include the Dublin Horse Show, drama and music festivals, the great rugby and hurling matches at Lansdowne Park, as stirring as any American football game. Enjoy the exquisite natural beauty, especially along the sweeping coastlines, the incredible architectural remnants of the past. (There are more Norman ruins in County Limerick alone than there are in Normandy, and Georgian Dublin is still the best-preserved eighteenth century in Europe. Visits to the Long Room in the Trinity College Library or to the Marino Casino near Howth Head are alone worth the price of a round-trip ticket to Ireland.)

You will be entering into one of the last of the never-never lands, a country overflowing with the good things of life—for the visitor—where time moves at a markedly slower pace than it does elsewhere and the unhurried inhabitants move in rhythm with the tempo. You will find yourself set down in a civilization which has been almost completely isolated since the beginning of history, set apart from the Roman conquest and the classical heritage, from the mainstream of Western thought, from the Renaissance and Reformation, the swirling philosophical tides which brought about the American, French, and Russian revolutions, and are still boiling across the face of the earth today.

Compensations as well as handicaps stem from such isolation. To the traveler a country where foreign affairs for a thousand years were limited primarily to invaders—Vikings, Normans, and English—visitors who bore with them flame and sword, cannonballs and crossbows, and where domestic affairs consisted mainly of efforts to resist those invaders, offers a past which is inseparable from the present. And for the traveler, today as always, what is more splendid than to be surrounded by the past?

But if you stay too long, and if like myself you had hoped to find that the native Irish were a newly freed nation which had set about creating a future worthy of their ancient glory and their recent accomplishments in other countries, you too will end up frustrated and disappointed. It will become apparent that the Irish, sunk in mediocrity and tilting with windmills, keeping up a gallant front to the rest of the world, have far less chance today, given the present set of conditions, than they had before the twenties of fulfilling what should be their rightful destiny. All unaware of it, they are more securely and strictly, what is worse, far more subtly imprisoned, more dependent on the will of others, than they ever were when the British ruled the land. If you stay, you too will begin to sigh for what might have been. And for what, perhaps, might still be.

In the chapters that follow, my own highly personal views on the current Irish situation are presented. From time to time I have also gone back into the past—the far-off legendary and preinvasion centuries of glory, as well as the recent bleak era of foreign oppression. Although this is not a history of Ireland, those historic events have been brought together which appear to have left a permanent mark, for better or worse, on the Irish.

After ten years in Ireland, I find much that happens there extremely paradoxical, but I believe my experiences will help you to understand more fully the country and the people. If there is any theme to this book, it is that the Irish, on the basis of evidence past and present, from inside and outside Ireland, should be doing far, far better than they are. That much of what is going on in Ireland today constitutes nothing more nor less than a national disgrace.

The longer one stays in Ireland the more one becomes aware of the devastation wrought during the past few centuries to the inner spirit of the Irish. This is truer of the men than the women, but every Roman Catholic in Ireland bears some scar, secretly or otherwise, which has resulted from the degradation inflicted on the race and creed. Nothing illustrated this more vividly than the visit to Ireland of the late President Kennedy. The Irish rose up to greet him in a massive, vibrating demonstration that was thrilling to behold. He afforded them a singular opportunity to express openly their inner conviction that they were the equals of any race on earth including their classic antagonists, the English. He soothed and nurtured a national psyche which has taken a nasty beating for many long, drab years.

This was in large measure the key to Kennedy's enormous popularity in Ireland. He was the only Irish-American who successfully bridged the gap in their hearts, not just because he was the President of the United States but because they saw in him a fellow Irishman who could move gracefully, affably, and naturally in all circles, in terms of politics, diplomacy, wealth, and society. He had pole-vaulted in one generation right over the heads of the English. It was comparable to the appeal Parnell had for so many of his countrymen.

Parnell wasn't bamboozled by, or in awe of, the English. He was a Protestant, a member of the landed gentry, educated at Cambridge, his mother an American, yet he always put the Irish people and their cause above everything else in his life. He appealed, like Kennedy, to all levels of the Irish. There is no more moving passage written by James Joyce than the scene in *A Portrait of the Artist as a Young Man* when at Christmas dinner his uncle, after a long bitter argument over Parnell, bows his head down on the table and cries out in anguish, "They have killed my king!" Catching the whole spirit of how the Irish masses reacted to Kennedy is a vignette from Sean O'Casey's *I Knock at the Door*, when he describes his mother being stopped in a horse-cab by a parade following Parnell through the streets of Dublin. The cabbie is speaking:

> That's Parnell himself that's passed, he said, when the cheering had subsided. Ireland's greatest son. I'd sell me hat, I'd sell me horse an' cab, I'd sell meself for him, be Jasus, I'd nearly sell me soul, if he beckoned me to do it.

What created a special bond of self-identification was President Kennedy's Roman Catholicism. When he was cut down in his prime, it was as though every family of that sect in Ireland had lost a son who had proved overseas the intrinsic worth of the Irish people. His photograph, alone or with his wife, still hangs in hundreds of thousands of kitchens and living rooms throughout Ireland. Even when he urged them in the Dáil to work in closer cooperation with the English, they applauded him, although a bit less enthusiastically.

It is the need for psychological reassurance on the part of the Irish which leads me to what has cast a perpetual cloud over these past eight years in Ireland. Within a matter of weeks I discovered to my dismay that the same ugly spirit of bigotry and intolerance so prevalent in New England forty years ago poisons the air of Ireland today. Nothing could have come as a deeper shock. It was the last thing I expected to find. Inconceivably the barriers within the Republic are raised not by the Irish Roman Catholic 95 percent of the population against the Anglo-Irish Protestant 5 percent of the population but by the 5 percent against the 95 percent. Between the two factions yawns an impassable chasm. I felt as though I had been carried upstream along a winding river and dropped down into an unpleasant scene from my New England boyhood.

For nearly ten years I have brooded over this preposterous situation, a distasteful anachronism not to be found in any other supposedly free and independent country except possibly one or two of the recently liberated African states. The alien ruling class from the days of captivity still flourishes in the Irish Republic. The British lion, toothless and mangy though he may have become at home and elsewhere, struts around the Irish scene, complete to jodhpurs and riding crop, as though he were still the supreme Lord of Creation.

Having assumed my own ecumenical stance some thirty years ago, being devoid of any formal church ties, with one child who is half-French and Roman Catholic and two children who are half-English and Protestant, my time has been spent about equally on each side of the chasm. If anything I have more close friends among the 5 percent. Living in the country, one can either commune solely with farmers, shopkeepers, and pub owners, mingle with the 5 percent, or dwell in solitude. In and around Dublin a few more people hop back and forth from one side to the other but a sharp division exists even there.

This unhappy situation creates such a feeling of empathy, complicates so many personal relationships, it would be pleasanter to skip the matter, but then it would be impossible to discuss modern Ireland. This hangover from the ghoulish past dovetails with several other major aspects of the present to such a degree that if it isn't discussed, the rest of Ireland today is unexplainable. These pages have been shown to a number of Irishmen and their wives, some educated outside the country, as well as to three foreigners living in Ireland. I wanted to be certain that out of some deep-seated frustration the situation was not being magnified. Without exception all of them felt the dimensions of the problem and its debilitating effects had been underplayed. A Protestant friend who has spent a good part of his time outside the country, added a neat twist by saying, "I wouldn't mind being a Roman Catholic anywhere else, but not in Ireland." So at least this isn't one biased man's opinion.

Far and away the most important question in modern Ireland is whether or not it is possible to create a broadly based society in which the various Christian sects can live and raise their children in harmony, as they do today except for color barriers in the United States and in England. Whatever other frightful problems beset these two countries, at least this question seems to have been settled for all time. In Ireland it seems highly unlikely that a comparable society will evolve during the foreseeable future. The Protestant Ascendancy in the Republic is only part of the story, but it provided me with my first and most unpleasant shock, so it might as well be discussed first.

Stretched across the twenty-six southern counties is an obtrusively evident gridwork of Protestant families and individuals whose blood is primarily English, whose daily lives, interests, and loyalties center almost entirely on themselves, their families, relations, friends, and on England. To the exclusion of anything Irish. To such a degree that one might be living in a British colony of a century ago. There are naturally daily contacts with the "natives," but they are the normal contacts of landowners with peasants and villagers.

It is surprising what an impact 5 percent of the population can make on the Irish scene. About 150,000 people. For one thing they have on the average more money than the native Irish. They live mainly on incomes ranging from modest to vast amounts, but some scrape along on next to nothing a year, while others live primarily on bank overdrafts against their property. Some are in Ireland because of a more favorable tax structure than in England.

More important in terms of their conspicuousness, they are primarily established in the "big houses," Georgian or otherwise, which until 1922 provided communal focal points comparable to the monasteries in earlier times and which in many cases still do this. Near most villages you will find one, two, three, or more of these houses in various degrees of repair or disrepair, usually situated on the best lands, providing trade for the village and employment for the locals. Near larger marketing centers such as Cork and Limerick the occupants buy on principle as much as possible from city enterprises owned and staffed by Protestants, of which there are still a goodly number.

Titles grow on every bush and stand out as special badges, since no titles are created by the Irish government. Although no new Irish titles have been created by the English government since 1922, except in the six northern counties, the inheritors of the old ones are still very much in evidence. It seems a bit odd until you get used to it to find people called "the Earl of Kerry," "the Countess of Donegal," "Lady Cork," or "Lord Tralee," wandering around in a supposed republic. A flock of English titles also graces the scene, and more arrive to stay each year.

The very fact that the Anglo-Irish are a closed shop makes them especially conspicuous. One locked door attracts far more attention than ten open ones, particularly when it's the biggest door in the neighborhood. Out of some three or four hundred people who move in what might be termed top social circles in Ireland, only four or five are Roman Catholic. There are scores of other attractive, charming, reasonably wealthy Irish Roman Catholics, both in town and country—not organized into a coherent laity but the potential leavenings of a New Society—to whom Anglo-Irish Protestant doors, as part of a firm and fixed principle of self-preservation, are shut tight.

Conversely, any English Protestants who come to live in the Irish countryside, even those you wouldn't cross the road to see in England, are more or less immediately accepted by the group, again as a matter of fixed principle. Aliens, in their own eyes surrounded by "alien corn," they welcome any newcomers from home. Thus, although there are some superb individual men and women in the group, the overall mixture, as is true of any clique set up on convoy lines, tends to be boring and mediocre, especially since one sees the same faces over and over again from one end of the Republic to the other.

At dinner on several occasions guests have discussed in low, shocked tones some dreadful tragedy that has befallen an Anglo-Irish Protestant family. Expecting to hear of a fatal motor accident or a forged-cheque charge, one learns instead that a son or daughter has become engaged to—a Roman Catholic! The consternation is similar to a Georgia plantation family which has just learned one of the children is planning an alliance of color.

Plunked down on much of the choicest land, the Anglo-Irish are wildly vociferous when any other nationalities purchase property in Ireland. This applies particularly to the Germans who are like needles in a haystack except in some parts of Kerry. Their attitudes toward most Americans—visitors, tenants, or landowners—is at best antisocial. An unsuspecting traveler from Long Island was recently approached by one of the more flamboyant females of the group whom he had never seen before.

"Why," she asked, "is an Irish-American like a worn-out bicycle seat?"

"You've got me," he replied. "Why?"

"Because they both give you a pain in the ass." She smiled, moving on to a more familiar huddle.

One writer from the past who would be extremely disappointed if he could return and see Ireland today would be William Bulfin whose *Rambles in Eirinn* appeared in 1907. Bulfin was most confident as to the eventual fate of the Protestant Ascendancy: "Standish O'Grady, one of themselves, and one of the best of them, told them the truth when he said they were going, going—'rotting from the land, without one brave word.' It is a terrible epitaph to write over the grave of a caste that might have been the glory and the salvation of the country."

After more than sixty years, the Anglo-Irish haven't gone. Nor do they appear to be going. Judging by the fact that about half of those one meets today were born in England, numerically things seem about as they were in 1922. The very fact they are far more of a minority percentagewise in the Republic, than they were before they were separated from the Protestants in the North, has driven them closer into each other's arms. With a few notable exceptions, from a positive standpoint they play a trivial role in Irish affairs.

No Dean Swift, no Wolfe Tone, no Charles Parnell, no John Mitchel, no Lord Edward Fitzgerald, no Bernard Shaw, no William Butler Yeats, no Oliver Goldsmith, no Laurence Sterne, no Oscar Wilde, no Henry Grattan, no Richard Brinsley Sheridan, no Robert Emmet, no Thomas Davis is present on the Irish scene today. These gigantic figures were all Protestants of English extraction, but above everything else they were Irishmen who helped immeasurably to make the Irish nation great.

Several years ago, the Protestant dean of St. Patrick's in Dublin told the younger members of his flock in effect that they should stop looking across the sea toward another country, should realize they are Irish citizens and should train themselves to participate actively in Irish affairs. To date there is no real evidence his words struck any more responsive chord in the rising Protestant generation than has been true of their parents.

One could be in Ireland for some time, visit the country fairly regularly, without becoming aware of the present Ascendancy status. Not too long ago one of the best-known U. S. newspapermen, himself an Irish-American who has often been in Ireland, asked me, "What is an Anglo-Irishman?" It was while looking for a house, first to rent, later to buy, that the situation was brought home to me. Some of the episodes have been forgotten. Others have stuck in my mind.

One afternoon I was talking to a mundane, middle-aged woman about a house on the sea north of

Dublin. In my innocence I happened to mention that my ancestors were Irish. "Oh," she said, surprised at my ignorance, "we're not *Irish*. We're *English*."

"Really?" I replied. "When did you come to Ireland?"

"Sometime in the eighteenth century," she answered.

"How do you like it?" I asked.

"Well," she said, "it's good and it's bad. The Irish are a shiftless lot. And we're always having to buy vegetables that are grown in Ireland even when they're more expensive. The cost of living's going up all the time. The government's a mess. It must have been a wonderful country fifty years ago. But there are a few nice people around if you know where to find them." My eyebrows stayed in a raised position for the next twenty-four hours, have never quite dropped all the way back into place.

One evening a few weeks later I received a telephone call from an elderly man I had met at lunch, a distinguished-looking colonel, retired from the British Army, rather a cold fish, English to the core in manner, dress, speech, although his family could trace its lineage back in Ireland to Strongbow's invasion. We are related by marriage—or we were. He has since joined Strongbow and the rest.

"I have just the house for you," he announced. "In County Meath. It's not yet on the market, but it will be soon. It was bought last year by a fellow from Dublin, but I think he's already found out that life in the country isn't for his kind. You'd like it though. After all, *you're one of us*."

The colonel had made a serious strategic error,

had allowed me a quick peep behind a curtain very few strangers even know exists. I hung up with a decidedly unpleasant sensation. I didn't like to think about the sort of treatment "the fellow from Dublin" was receiving, in his own country at the hands of his County Meath neighbors. For the first time since I could remember, I thought back to my own beginnings and then of their implications in modern Ireland. "For whom *does* the bell toll?" I asked myself. I knew I would always be *them,* not *us,* that I could never deny myself or my own people. Thirty-five years earlier I had fled from the transplanted Irish of New England. Now I had run around in a great circle and all unawares had ended up back at the very heart of the matter.

That same week I looked at two houses less than a mile apart in County Wicklow. The first was owned by an Irish Roman Catholic widow with two particularly attractive young children, the other by an Anglo-Irish family whose name has played a prominent role in Irish history. They were the only two "big houses" in the neighborhood. I mentioned to the second woman that the first woman was ill in bed, that her older child had shown me through the house. "I know," she replied, "she's been ill a great deal. I should have called on her, but somehow I've never got around to meeting her." The other woman had owned her home for seven years.

A few weeks later a charming Anglo-Irishwoman whose house we were looking at in County Cork said, "You won't have any trouble with the locals. Oh, once in a while they paint an insulting sign on our wall but in general they don't seem to mind us too much." I wondered whether the true feelings in that particular village had changed materially since the Troubles.

About this same time, due mainly to the efforts of the *Sunday Independent* newspaper, Roman Catholic Tommy Wade and his celebrated horse Dumdrum (religion unspecified) were shoved over the bars of discrimination onto the Irish Equestrian Team. They won thrilling victories against competitors from all parts of the world. This had been in a sense a double discrimination since Dumdrum, before he was bought and trained by Tommy Wade, had for a short time pulled a milk cart. To the Anglo-Irish his breeding was as suspect as Tommy Wade's.

The overall sports situation has improved perceptibly. Before 1922 few if any native Roman Catholics made the All-Ireland Rugby Team. Now they do, although the GAA (the Gaelic Athletic Association) still forbids its members to play either of the two "foreign" (i.e., British) sports, rugby and cricket. Even as popular a figure as Donough O'Malley, the late Minister for Education, whose death at forty-seven was a tragic loss for Ireland, was emphatically voted down when he spoke out against "the Ban." During the past few decades the Roman Catholics have invaded the golf clubs, which accounts for a large number of the Anglo-Irish losing their former zest for the game. As for hurling—no self-respecting Anglo-Irishman would be caught dead watching *that* native sport, which somehow survived the Statutes of Kilkenny outlawing it in the fourteenth century.

In the small County Kildare village where we finally rented a house there were two or three Anglo-

Irish Protestant families and twenty or thirty Irish Roman Catholic families. One Catholic couple and one Protestant couple became particularly close friends of ours. During the following year on a number of occasions we introduced the two couples to one another. The Protestant couple always acted as though they had never met the other man and his wife. I finally asked the Catholic husband, "What happens, Jim, if you meet the So-and-sos or the So-and-sos (mentioning another Anglo-Irish couple) in the village or at the races or in Dublin?"

"Oh, sure," laughed Jim in deprecating fashion. "I gave up on that long ago. Once in a while they speak. Usually they don't. So now if they say hello, I say hello. If they don't, I don't."

All of this may sound petty and trivial to someone in the outside world, torn as it is by more violent if not more ancient antagonisms. But when the daily episodes I have time and again witnessed firsthand are multiplied over and over in practically every rural area, every village and small town in the Republic, in Limerick, Cork, and even in Dublin, it not only seems like a spectacularly un-Christian way for neighbors to live together, but by keeping open old wounds it seriously hampers the kind of close relationship which, as never before, is so vitally needed between England and Ireland. In its own insidious fashion it also slows down drastically, through the maintenance of a psychological Border, the progress of the Irish nation.

Contained within the attitude of the Anglo-Irish toward the Irish is one of the major reasons why disaster has overtaken the British Empire in so many parts of the world. Reading of King Edward VII's visit to India as Prince of Wales, before the turn of the century, of his indignation and amazement at the colonials' treatment of the native Indians, of the colonials' savage antagonism toward Edward because of his "fraternizing" with the natives, one can presage the inevitable loss to the empire of India. This is history now, but in Ireland, the Anglo-Irish are a part of current events, and they badly complicate a messy, deeply imbedded situation. One of the London Sunday newspapers last year spoke of the bitterness instilled in so many "native" hearts by British colonials, of Jomo Kenyatta as one key African figure whose initial opposition to Britain grew directly out of unpleasant personal experiences. While not a "native," General De Gaulle is obviously another person who "got the treatment" from the English, out of which stems many of England's current problems with the Continent.

The present situation in the Irish Republic is further complicated by the fact that the rigid, highly class-conscious, closed-shop Anglo-Irish gridwork of bigotry is set down squarely on top of the least class-conscious, least snobbish, most unbourgeois and democratic society in Western Europe. No one who has spent much time in Ireland will quarrel with this definition. When one observes the two diametrically opposed social patterns—native Irish and Anglo-Irish—cheek by jowl today, one realizes how much of the trouble during the past three hundred years arose because the Irish resented the English upper classes doing to them what they so successfully did to their own less fortunate fellow countrymen in England. In the nineteenth century a bottle of gin was the quickest way out of Glasgow, Cardiff, *and* Dublin, as well as Manchester. Dublin finally substituted the rifle for the bottle.

In trying to maintain their Ascendancy over the Irish the Anglo-Irish may feel they are somehow helping England's cause in Ireland. They are in truth doing the direct opposite. By their daily actions and attitudes they serve as perpetual, ever-present ambassadors of ill will, constant reminders of the unforgotten past. The British government, after a careful screening, could well afford to pay many of them to leave Ireland and return to what they secretly or openly consider their true home.

The dreariest aspect of the Anglo-Irish facet of Irish society is that their very physical presence helps retard the normal development of a truly intellectual, liberal, broad-minded group of national secular leaders comparable to what exists in other Western countries. Through self-imposed segregation and because of inverted interests the Protestant Anglo-Irish at best suffer from atrophy, at worst represent a social and cultural fifth column. The native Roman Catholics in turn are stunted by frustrations, rebuffs, lack of education, and their own parochial limitations. If they would try, the Anglo-Irishman could help the Irish Roman Catholics escape from their own strictures, self-imposed or otherwise. There are additional key reasons for the lack of a strong Roman Catholic laity in Ireland, but the fact that a vacuum tends to fill itself and that thanks to the Anglo-Irish there is no such vacuum at the top, must be weighted heavily as one major cause of the Republic being today, except for her churchmen and politicians, a leaderless nation.

One has to hand it to the Anglo-Irish. They are a tough bunch. Every bit as tough, tenacious, and indestructible as the native Irish. Perhaps the country breeds toughness. The Anglo-Irish survived in the twenties, their eleventh hour. And their twelfth. Unfortunately the bulk of them—and again I must apologize to the splendid exceptions—have learned nothing from the past. One still hears them, wrapped in their moth-eaten exclusiveness, refer ad nauseam to the native Irish as "shiftless, insincere, lazy, white niggers, drunken, superstitious, quarrelsome, dishonest, ungrateful, deceitful—amusing and gay, yes, quick-witted, yes, but totally incapable of running their own affairs, etc., etc., etc." These are still the private opinions of the Anglo-Irish. On and on and on until the decanter of port has circled the polished mahogany table for the last time, the last cheroot has been tossed into the Adam fireplace, the last pair of horse-bowed, dinner-jacketed legs has teetered out into the silent, unanswering Irish night, to the waiting Land Rover.

Some may wonder why William Butler Yeats is included in the very top echelon of Irish immortals. He is there not only because above anyone else he brought back into the sunlight Ireland's dimly remembered past, but even more because when the moment of supreme truth arrived he, an Anglo-Irish Protestant, saw for the first time that the common Irish around him in the flesh were the equals in every way of those whose epic spirits had long enthralled and inspired him. Not only saw the truth sooner and more fully than most of the native Irish but set it down on September 25, 1916, for all the world to read and remember:

*I have met them at close of day*
*Coming with vivid faces*
*From counter or desk among grey*
*Eighteenth-century houses.*
*I have passed with a nod of the head*
*Or polite meaningless words,*
*Or have lingered awhile and said*
*Polite meaningless words,*
*And thought before I had done*
*Of a mocking tale or a gibe*
*To please a companion*
*Around the fire at the club,*
*Being certain that they and I*
*But lived where motley is worn:*
*All changed, changed utterly:*
*A terrible beauty is born.*

Those who have stood at the bar in the Kildare Street Club or the Shelbourne Hotel, who have dined in county houses and listened to the endless episodes from the lives of Paddy and Mick, of Norah and Bridget, will appreciate the white-hot, self-accusing irony of those lines:

*And thought before I had done*
*Of a mocking tale or a gibe*
*To please a companion*
*Around the fire at the club,*

*Being certain that they and I*
*But lived where motley is worn.*

A terrible beauty was, indeed, born in Ireland at Easter time, 1916. But after more than half a century the Anglo-Irish still haven't recognized her socially.

In my mind's eye I see a large motor bus careening along a narrow, dusty road. The driver is intent on his job. Most of the occupants are reading newspapers, looking out the windows, dozing, smoking, chatting quietly back and forth. Only occasionally does one of them glance casually at two men who are on the floor in the aisle of the bus.

One of the men lies flat on his face. The other sits astride his back, beating him savagely with a heavy club about the head and shoulders. The man below, with a superhuman effort, finally struggles to his feet. Clothing torn, bruised, and bloody, he turns and faces his assailant.

The man with the club partially conceals it behind his back with his left hand, breaks into a broad, toothy grin, holds out his right hand, and says, "Let's be friends. Let's forget what's happened. After all, we're living in a civilized world. Let's shake on it." At the same time he places one hobnailed boot squarely on the other man's bare foot and steps down on it just as hard as he can.

The other man accepts the outstretched hand and in spite of the excruciating pain tries to smile. "Fair enough," he replies. "Let bygones be bygones. But, ah, do you mind getting off my foot?"

"What's that?" asks the first man, exposing a few more molars and pretending not to hear, leaning forward and grinding his boot down harder. "What did you say, Old Chap?"

"You're standing on my foot," explains the other man. "It hurts. Do you mind getting off?" By now his foot is mangled and bleeding.

"Well! Can you beat that?" The man with the club, his boot still tightly clamped down, turns to the other occupants of the bus. "Here I'm trying to be friends, and this fellow is spoiling for a fight."

"He seems a rather shoddy sort," agrees one of the onlookers, gazing over his newspaper. "And he does have a reputation for being a troublemaker. If he doesn't behave himself, why don't you knock a little sense into him with that club?"

"I'd hate to have to do it," replies the clubman with a regretful shake of his head. "But I certainly will if he tries to start something."

Those familiar with current events in Ireland, who know that the North is still part of the United Kingdom, will have no trouble identifying the two main characters in this little allegory. For other readers here are two small hints: The man with the club isn't Ireland. And the fellow whose foot is being stepped on isn't England.

Not long after coming here I was sitting in the office of a gentle, highly respected solicitor, a pillar of his community, the sort of person who brushes a fly off his desk rather than kill it. We were discussing the Border and the immediate events leading up to Partition. "Of course," he said, looking up at the ceiling, "you realize there's only one way we'll ever get back the Six Counties?"

"How's that?" I asked.

"The same way we got the Republic," he replied. "With a gun."

During the years that have followed, although Unionist politicians in the North are constantly reassuring themselves, their constituents, the Irish, the English, and the outside world that south of the Border only a few "hotheads," "gangsters," "terrorists," and "gunmen"—the identical terms used during the Troubles—believe any longer in "violence," I have discovered most average citizens in the Republic are convinced force will provide the final solution. Many regret this is true and want no part of it. The majority, since they have never observed the English yielding an inch to anyone anywhere except under pressure, think it is the inevitable conclusion to this last, unfinished chapter in a disastrous relationship, the one way to remove the major obstacle to what could be a mutually beneficial partnership between the English and the Irish. I report this to those outside so they won't be too surprised some morning to pick up their newspapers or turn on their TV sets and find out that all hell has broken out again in Ireland.

About the time of that conversation—possibly the cause of it—a member of the Royal Ulster Constabulary was shot in a raid on the Border, the last such occurrence. The next day the Irish edition of the London *Daily Mail* carried a front-page banner headline: "END OF PARTITION PUT BACK TEN YEARS!"

Aha! I said to myself, then a date *has* been set. Reading through the article, I couldn't find one. As soon as things quieted down, the Northern politicians went back to saying what they had been saying all along: Partition is here to stay. Only a fortnight ago Captain Terence O'Neill, Prime Minister of Northern Ireland, on the retirement of the former prime minister from the Northern House of Commons, declared, "When Lord Brookborough entered political life, many hazards beset the infant state of Northern Ireland. His enduring achievement is the existence of a thriving province whose position within the United Kingdom is no longer in doubt."

Quite a cry from "end of partition put back ten years." One can hardly blame the Irish people for being cynical as to how far peaceful means will ever get them. The fact that "the thriving province" of the United Kingdom happens to be a large portion of the same Ulster Province which for over two thousand years was an integral part of Ireland doesn't seem to bother Captain O'Neill. As a loyal servant of the Queen of England, he is bound by his Orange Order oath to support her as long as she supports the Protestant Ascendancy in Ireland, or at least in the part where the Crown still has jurisdiction.

(The Orange Order came into being on the day of the notorious battle of the Diamond, September 21, 1795, the first serious engagement fought between native Irish Catholics and Protestants. The purpose of the Order: "To maintain the laws and peace of the country and the Protestant Constitution and to defend the King and his heirs as long as they shall maintain the Protestant ascendancy."

(The order spread rapidly throughout Ireland, reaching a membership of 125,000, but after a series of outrages it was banned only to be revived again in 1845. Today this same institution with the same original purpose is the real boss of Northern Ireland. Captain O'Neill and his entire cabinet are leading, active members, providing the hard core of the Unionist Party which has been in power at Stormont, the Northern seat of government, with an overwhelming majority every year since Ireland was partitioned. All but two of the Unionist members of the Northern House of Commons are members of the Orange Order, and their two seats are about to be abolished.)

Aside from the fact that Ulster has been stolen from the Irish people, what has happened there for the past forty-six years and is still happening constitutes as disagreeable a situation as many which existed during the past several centuries. Two thirds of the population, Protestants, mainly of English and Scottish extraction, through a well-rounded program of political skulduggery, discrimination, bigotry, and Ku-Klux-Klanlike intimidation, with the bully boys in this instance backed up by the Royal Irish Constabulary and the British armed forces, systematically cheat the Irish Roman Catholic third of the population—actually about 36 percent—out of their supposedly inalienable rights as British subjects.

Which is over and above the fundamental fact that

this group of more than half a million people are Irish men, women, and children living on the same soil where their ancestors have lived since before the dawn of history. The Ulster Plantation started as a swindle of the Irish people and that a swindle is still being perpetrated is obvious to anyone who has even casually perused the local news during the past few years. Due primarily to the disconcerting glare of publicity set off by rioting two years ago, the Unionist leaders, tucking their Orange Order robes away for the moment in a dark closet, have been positively oozing with protestations of brotherly love and promises of better days to come. To date not one single step has been taken to correct the situation.

Most of the ugly news slips out in spite of tight government "supervision" backed up by wholehearted cooperation from police officers, the judiciary, and other interested officials, many of whom are themselves members of the Orange Order. The most revealing picture of conditions was painted in a series of articles which ran in the *Irish Sunday Independent*, written by T. P. Kilfeather, a hard-hitting, straightforward reporter who has kindly given permission to include some of the highlights from the series herein.

Although 36 percent of the total population in Northern Ireland is Roman Catholic, less than 4 percent of state- and semistate-appointed positions are filled by Roman Catholics.

Typical of conditions throughout the Six Counties is what goes on in Derry City which Mr. Kilfeather used as his principal example. Here there are 32,000 Nationalist (Roman Catholic) electors and 18,000 Unionist (Protestant) electors. In spite of being outnumbered almost two to one, the Unionists obtain each year an overwhelming majority on the Derry City Council. The method used would make an old-time Tammany Hall ward heeler blush with shame.

The city is divided into four wards. The city council controls house building. In municipal housing schemes the Roman Catholics are allotted houses in only one ward, the so-called Catholic ward. They are not allowed to become tenants of a city-owned house in the three so-called Protestant wards. Thus, in spite of their huge voting plurality, as far as membership on the all-important city council is concerned, the Roman Catholics are outnumbered three to one. Not being able to get control of the city council, they have never been able to change the housing allocation.

(This is a somewhat worse situation than the one in Newark, New Jersey, where through a comparable scheme the slightly more than 50 percent nonwhite population is limited to two out of the nine seats on the city council. As of the moment it appears that the setup in Newark will be rectified long before the one in Derry City.)

In order to make voting figures more plausible and to preserve the status quo, the Derry City Council enlarged one ward to take in villages deep in the surrounding rural area where the population is predominantly Protestant. This type of gerrymandering is standard practice throughout the Six Counties and has been ever since Partition began.

Not one Roman Catholic is employed on the executive or office staff of the Derry City Council. The Unionists protest loudly that they don't ask job applicants to state their religion, that selection is made purely on the basis of merit. They do, however, require that schools attended must be listed. In the Six Counties this is equivalent to stating one's religion, and again this is standard practice everywhere, in private industry, for domestic staff and farm jobs, as well as state, county, and municipal appointments.

Recently it came out that in County Fermanagh, where Roman Catholics outnumber Protestants, not one of the seventy school bus drivers is a Roman Catholic. Just before his retirement from the Northern House of Commons, Lord Brookborough, now over eighty, said he was sorry that some forty years ago he had announced that Protestants shouldn't hire Catholics *in any capacity*. It seems a pity his lordship couldn't have spoken up a bit sooner or that some of his younger, more active fellow Orangemen have nothing to say on this politically delicate matter. At the moment they are busily engaged in ejecting from their ranks a prominent member who bears the same first and last names as one of the great seventeenth-century Irish patriots, Phelim O'Neill. His crime—attending a Roman Catholic wedding ceremony!

Coming back to Derry, the same pattern that dominates the housing situation prevails in private industry which is largely owned by Protestants. A Roman Catholic, no matter what technical qualifications he may have, is rarely if ever employed in an executive capacity. This process continues right down the line. It is a hard-and-fast unwritten rule that no Catholic is ever hired for even the most menial job if a Protestant is available. As a result thousands of Derry Roman Catholic workers have had to migrate to England in search of work, which naturally suits the Protestant minority because it reduces the Catholic majority. There is a second side benefit. Derry is a center of the shirt-making industry. "If Derry men cannot get work," states Mr. Kilfeather, "their wives and daughters must go to work in the shirt factories to provide food, rent, and fuel." This also suits the Protestant owners since it provides a ready source for sweatshop labor.

A traditional sore spot has been the Mater Hospital in Belfast. This is a famous institution run by the Sisters of Mercy. Anyone, irrespective of religion, is admitted. Although other hospitals receive thousands of pounds in state aid, the Unionist government has consistently refused to grant one shilling to the Mater.

As far as representation in the British House of Commons is concerned, here is the picture as summarized in the *Irish Independent*:

> All the election wards are gerrymandered in the Six Counties.
>
> Northern Ireland sends twelve members to the British Parliament at Westminster, London.
>
> The majority votes which the Protestant (Unionist) members of this parliament receive astonish English, Welsh, and Scottish members at Westminster.
>
> Two of these MPs have majorities of more than 50,000, one has more than 40,000, another more than 30,000. Four of them have more than 20,000, and three have more than 10,000. Only one of the twelve has less than a majority of 10,000.

These majorities are fantastic. In Britain seats are often won or lost by two, three, or four votes.

*The Northern Ireland majorities are obtained at election times by the simple system of arranging constituencies so that each of them will have a huge Protestant vote.* A "Ghetto" system enables the Unionists to retain unchallenged power and special privilege.

There has been *not one change* in the government of the Six Counties since Ireland was partitioned forty-five years ago. This is unique in all Europe and is possibly a world record.

How would the Republicans feel in the United States if the Democrats were able to "rig" the elections so that there would always be a Democratic President, Senate, and House of Representatives over a period of forty-five years?

This is what has happened in the Six Counties.

The position of England in relationship to Northern Ireland and Partition is becoming an increasingly tricky one. Today no real quarrel exists between England and Ireland. Many sane people on both sides of the Irish Sea are beginning to realize their individual well-being depends on their mutual well-being. About 65 percent of the tourist money spent in the Irish Republic each year comes from England. More and more of the English cross over each summer on their holidays and find a warm welcome waiting for them. During the past eight years not one unfortunate incident has occurred between these former adversaries.

At Westminster the fact that the Unionist bloc is an integral part of the Conservative Party has given the Labour Government pause for reflection. The same chicanery that operates against the Roman

Catholics north of the Border also operates against the Labour Party. Individual MPs, some Roman Catholic and/or of Irish descent but others as well, have begun to raise embarrassing questions as to what is going on in the North of Ireland. The Unionists, although they are constantly engaging themselves in English affairs, stoutly maintain these questions are internal matters and must be handled at Stormont, not at Westminster. But this is a wobbly tightrope.

Recently it was revealed that the Special Powers Act in Northern Ireland seriously compromises Great Britain's position as far as the United Nations' Charter of Human Rights is concerned. It is possible that in the years ahead a situation roughly parallel to Rhodesia may develop, where the English will refuse to support or condone what is being done by the Orange Order and the Unionists, in which case Stormont might try to go it alone. At the same time, in the last analysis Partition and the Border wouldn't exist in Ireland today if it hadn't been for Great Britain, and it is only the backup by the British armed forces that allows the situation to continue. As long as this is true, England cannot smile benignly at Stormont and Dublin, and with a nod of sympathy say, "It's your local problem, boys. You settle it." There is also the equally important question whether the taxpayers in the United Kingdom can afford to go on paying for what has become an outmoded political luxury whose benefits are increasingly dubious.

During the past two years the question of what should be done in the future about the Roman Catholics in Northern Ireland has started to cause cracks in the heretofore monolithic Unionist Party. A number of viciously quarrelsome factions have been tugging back and forth with one another. This infighting has revealed to the outside world far more effectively than could have been done by any impartial body the miserable plight of the Northern Irish Catholics. The shock has been severe to a large, fair-minded portion of the English home population. None of the factions has been able, or has even bothered, to cover up what *has* been going on. The question is, What should be done in the years ahead?

The reason for the split is a simple one. At the present rate of growth, within the next twenty or twenty-five years, the Roman Catholic *minority*—unless the government resorts to old-time deportations or plantations—will have become a *majority*. (There are some indications that the present figure of 36 percent is rigged on the downward side.) This specter of things to come has tossed the Unionists/Orangemen onto the horns of one of those nasty dilemmas which have an awkward habit of emerging in Ireland:

*Should the Unionists start to play ball with the Roman Catholics right now, in the hope that through some actual concessions blown up with good, old-fashioned hot air, the Catholics will in twenty years have forgotten the past and be content to support the Union with Great Britain?*

*Or should the Protestants continue to squash the Catholics under, continue to bulldoze them out of their rights to an equitable share in the management of affairs, leaving the long-term problems to the next generation, as has been done so often and so disastrously in the past?*

The factions in the six northern counties today

range from an extremely noisy, militant, group who have rallied around the standard of a rabble-rousing, self-styled Man of God, a correspondence-school minister named Ian Paisley, all the way through varying shades of opinion to a handful of Protestants who are nonmembers of the Orange Order and who believe the ecumenical spirit must, in the long run, prevail in the six counties along with the rest of the Christian world. Active in this last group are a number of Church of Ireland ministers who are in an especially uncomfortable position since many of the most prominent members of their flock are Unionists and Orange Lodge members.

The Paisleyites as well as a goodly portion of the middle grounders are intense in their conviction that, right now as never before, the Roman Catholics must be crushed down. On numerous occasions they have resorted to violence, including at least one proved case of murder. Every week or so items slip through into the newspapers which tell of Protestant parents who have been beaten up for allowing their daughters to date Roman Catholic boys, of Roman Catholics who have been subjected to round-the-clock intimidation for daring to move into Protestant neighborhoods, of Orangemen who have been expelled for attending Roman Catholic weddings, funerals, and christenings. Many other similar occurrences never make the newspapers at all.

That the bulk of the northern Protestants stand far closer in sympathy to Paisley than to the Church of Ireland ministers was dramatically revealed by a series of disgraceful episodes which took place on the Twelfth of July in 1967, the anniversary of the battle of the Boyne, incidents which must have made William of Orange turn over in his grave. The most appalling happened in Belfast. A contingent of Orangemen, on their way to join the annual parade, marched past the Crumlin Street Jail where two followers of Paisley, *still members of the Orange Order*, are serving life sentences for murdering a Catholic.

The marchers were accompanied by a member of the Stormont Parliament. They stopped and sent in a message of hearty "fraternal salutations" to the two lifers, as well as to a third Orangeman who is serving a long term for a crime of violence. The messages were duly passed on by the prison authorities. To make matters much worse, the Unionist Minister for Home Affairs, William Craig, announced that "fraternal salutations" do not necessarily imply the condoning of murder. He further brought down the wrath of labor-union leaders by stating in a parliamentary speech that "this sort of thing goes on all the time between labor leaders and their members!"

Elsewhere on the same festive day speakers were beaten up—in one case a well-known MP had to be hospitalized—for advising Orangemen to follow Captain O'Neill's advice and "be nice to the Catholics." At a number of other meetings the oath of allegiance to the Prime Minister was omitted from the schedule. The overwhelming impression was that a large majority of the Orangemen were dead set against even the outward amenities as far as Catholics are concerned. As of this moment it would appear that, if anything, things will get worse rather than better.

As this book goes to press, things have already gotten much worse. During October, 1968, there were several days of rioting and bloodshed in Derry City, and on December 2, in Armagh—the religious capital for both Roman Catholic and Protestant churches—the true situation in Northern Ireland was exposed to daylight in all its naked force.

Having been given permission to parade peacefully through the streets of the city, five thousand Civil Rights marchers were confronted by two thousand Paisleyites. Here is what happened, as stated in George Devlin's report to the *Irish Independent*:

> Three hundred police surrendered power to armed bands of Paisleyites who, from noon, held the city centre against the Rights marchers. The police publicly admitted their inability to keep the march route open. . . .
>
> The Civil Rights march was due to begin at 2:30 P.M. but Rev. Ian Paisley and members of the Ulster Constitutional Defense Committee took up positions in Thomas Street, about the center of the proposed parade route, twelve hours earlier. By noon about two thousand of his hymn-singing followers were blocking the streets.
>
> They could be identified by blue lapel buttons. Many wore crash helmets and brandished legs of tables and heavy pieces of wood, topped with nails. Reporters were told to "clear off." Cameramen were told not to take pictures or their equipment would be smashed. . . .
>
> Mr. Brian McRoberts, an Armagh solicitor and the prospective official Unionist candidate for West Belfast . . . was attacked by Paisleyites in the Market Square area after they had thumped his car with broom handles, howling "O'Neill must go."

Mr. McRoberts got out and told them he would not be intimidated by anyone. He was beaten, knocked down and kicked. Two policemen rescued him.

Rev. Mr. Ian Paisley, who was carrying a blackthorn stick, alleged that Mr. McRoberts had tried to drive through the crowds to provoke them.

Held in check by their stewards, the Civil Rights group finally abandoned the march.

The Paisleyites then swaggered on a victory parade through the city centre, arrogantly swinging their cudgels. Rev. Mr. Paisley announced that "the enemy has been routed."

In the Mall, they attacked an I.T.N. cameraman, Mr. Ken Taylor, of Reigate, Surrey, clubbing him to the ground. When a local resident tried to rescue Mr. Taylor the mob turned on him.

After stalking the streets for more than an hour the mob gradually melted. As about twenty Paisleyites marched with a Union Jack to their buses at Cathedral Road they clashed with a group of young people.

Stones and bottles shattered windows of the two buses and steel helmeted police, carrying shields, baton-charged the group of young people, who retaliated with stones. Several, including a girl, fell.

Minutes later a B.B.C. TV crew was attacked by police at Upper English Street. A reporter, Mr. Richard Kershaw, said they had filmed the incidents at Cathedral Road when they were punched by about five R.U.C. men who smashed their £3,000 camera.

Mr. Kershaw added that he had been struck on the knee with a baton and that another member of the unit had been punched in the face. He said the team had not been provocative to the police.

That night Mr. Paul Rose, a prominent member of the English Houses of Parliament called for the removal of Captain William Craig, Unionist Minister for Home Affairs, who recently referred to the Irish Roman Catholics as "Rogues and Rascals." "It is quite obvious," stated Mr. Rose, "that Craig and his supporters are resisting any reform in northern Ireland."

The same night Mr. Edward McAteer, M.P., the Nationalist parliamentary leader in Northern Ireland, asked: "What is the state of the law now? Are the police now content to disperse peaceful demonstrators and give free rein to shillelagh-armed Government supporters, assembled in open defiance of the law? Is it simply jungle law from now on?"

Two weeks later there has been no government condemnation of either the Paisleyites or the Royal Ulster Constabulary, the northern Ireland police force. But the Protestant Archbishop of Armagh, the Most Reverend Dr. McCann, head of the Church of Ireland throughout the entire country, made it clear where the vast majority of the Unionists' sympathies lie when he stated:

"I would like to thank the officers and men of the R.U.C. for their magnificent work in keeping the peace and for the strain under which they had to perform their duties.

"We thank God that things were not worse and that the police were able to keep the turbulent elements under control."

Apparently Archbishop McCann still shares the view held universally by the Ascendancy throughout Ireland for the past few centuries (but not publicly expressed too loudly these days south of the Border) that almighty God is on the side of the Irish Protestants.

What baffles the imagination is that Captain O'Neill, the northern Prime Minister (whose name in the ordinary course of human events should not be O'Neill but Chichester, since an ancestor of his by that name married a Miss O'Neill and then changed his name) has the affrontery to pay periodic visits to the United States, seeking out American firms, many of them owned and/or managed by Roman Catholics, to invest money in his part of the world.

Or that Mr. Aristotle Onassis, husband of the former wife of the late John F. Kennedy, in the greatest single shot-in-the-arm given the Unionists during the past decade, should lend without any strings attached £25,000,000 to the Belfast ship-building firm of Harland and Wolff.

After eight years in Ireland it becomes apparent that what the Unionists fear most is (1) publicity and (2) that the Roman Catholics in America will boycott and bring pressure to bear against them until the situation is righted.

I find myself thinking of three young Irish Roman Catholics of the last century who were born within a twenty-mile radius of one another in northern Ireland:

Charles Russell migrated as a struggling barrister from Belfast to London in 1860. He became Lord Chief Justice of England.

Charles Gavan Duffy, a founder and editor of *The Nation*, after a dramatic career fighting for Irish

Independence, was deported for life to Australia. He became Prime Minister of Victoria.

Thomas D'Arcy McGee, poet, journalist, member of the rebel Irish war council of '48, left in despair for North America. He became Canada's Minister of Agriculture.

I wonder what would have happened to those three young Catholic neighbors if they had stayed at home in northern Ireland. More pertinent, I wonder what would be happening to them if they lived in Northern Ireland today. Who can say how many young men, with comparable talents, are living and dying in obscurity among the dank weeds of bigotry and discrimination that choke the Northern Irish scene at this very moment? At a time when intelligence and energy have never been so badly needed in this part of the world. It would seem that the only logical choice for any young Roman Catholic in present-day Northern Ireland lies between a rifle and a bottle of whiskey or a one-way ticket to the outside world.

Recently Captain O'Neill asked the Republican Irish to apply "realism" to the current situation. He severely criticized *The Irish Times,* the most Anglo-Irish newspaper in the South, for stating editorially that it would be highly desirable if soon once again the spirit of Wolfe Tone and Robert Emmet, both Irish Protestant martyrs for freedom, might pervade the Northern atmosphere. He asked further that both sides "emasculate" themselves of sentiment and tradition. What it came down to was that his "realism" consists entirely of the fact that for nearly fifty years Ulster has been partitioned from the rest of Ireland, which appears to be a pinpoint in the overall historic panorama. While Captain O'Neill may carve out a niche for himself as the Great Emasculator in British history, he is hardly likely to do so in Irish history, which is only fair enough. As Gavan Duffy said a century ago, "No man can have more than one mother country."

Elsewhere in the same speech Captain O'Neill said that the native Irish Roman Catholics and the Protestants in the North were bound to have their own particular objects of veneration—that you could hardly expect the native Irish to carry Queen Victoria's banner in a parade. Here he was being totally unrealistic, as he would quickly discover if he strolled through the streets and public squares of Dublin. On the main thoroughfare, between the statues of the Protestant Anglo-Irish-American Parnell, and the native Irish Roman Catholic, Daniel O'Connell, stands the stocky figure of the great Irish temperance leader, Father Theobald Mathew, who was descended from a Cromwellian Protestant soldier. Even more pertinent, the three glorious memorials erected *during the past year* in St. Stephen's Green in Dublin are all to Anglo-Irish Protestants—Emmet, Tone, and William Butler Yeats.

On a broader level there *is* one reality which has materially affected relationships between the English and the Irish in the past and will continue to affect them until the end of time. For better or worse, for richer or poorer, the two islands are in juxtaposition to one another, semi-isolated from the rest of Europe. Most of those in Ireland who feel that the nation should be reunited *politically* are the first to agree that in return, simultaneously, a closer form of *economic* partnership should be worked out with the United Kingdom. Most of these same people would be willing to have a united Ireland reenter the British Commonwealth or some comparable form of mutual association.

Looking ahead twenty-five years, it would seem that—whether or not Great Britain and Ireland enter the Common Market, which at the moment looks unlikely—for the good of everyone in England, Ireland, Scotland, and Wales some sort of *regional* planning group should immediately be set up to explore long-term avenues leading to overall benefits. One of the most irrational aspects of Partition was that it divided the essentially industrial North from the essentially agricultural South. As a result each part has been struggling for almost half a century to achieve a balanced internal economy without any relationship to the other part or to the overall picture in the twin islands.

It will be a pity if the reunification of Ireland takes place without the Irish Protestants playing an active role, but with or without them it is bound to happen. While it is devoutly to be hoped that rational thinking and understanding will prevail, let no one be mistaken that at this very moment, in the hearts and minds of many young voiceless Irishmen, the lines written by Padraic Pearse in his poem "The Rebel"—Pearse who in the following year wrote the Irish declaration of independence—apply equally to Northern Ireland today as they did to all of Ireland in 1916. This is every bit as much of a "reality" as something that can be seen or touched or smelled or tasted or heard. More of a reality in terms of human destiny.

I have talked to enough young Irish people, especially in the villages and on farms, to know that the spirit which moved Pearse to write these lines is not dead, and who can honestly say, reflecting on the entrenched Orangemen of the North and the unregenerate Protestant Ascendancy in the South, that such a spirit should ever die?

> *And I say to my people's masters: Beware,*
> *Beware of the thing that is coming,*
> *beware of the risen people,*
> *Who shall take what ye would not give.*
> *Did ye think to conquer the*
> *people,*
> *Or that Law is stronger than life and*
> *than men's desire to be free?*
> *We will try it out with you, ye that have*
> *harried and held,*
> *Ye that have bullied and bribed, tyrants,*
> *hypocrites.*

In modern Ireland a steady flow of somewhat hazy propaganda emanates from north of the Border and is occasionally echoed within the Republic, which tries to create the impression that Ulster has always been "Separatist," less Irish and Roman Catholic than the rest of the country, more loyal by instinct and tradition to the Crown. This has been successful to the extent that today about half the people in the South believe it's true. The facts show quite a different picture.

In the sixteenth century Ulster held out until the end against England, the last province to surrender, remaining staunchly Catholic until the closing years of the century. During the seventeenth and eighteenth centuries and well into the nineteenth, she played the key role in the fight to regain independence, contributing by far the largest number of great leaders to the cause, *both Catholics and Protestants*. Even when the tides of plantation and migration, plus the fanning of religious differences, changed the overall picture, it was still the Protestants from Belfast and elsewhere who in the main, while the Roman Catholics lay prostrate and silent, kept the flame of nationalism burning right up until 1916. Nowhere is this made clearer than in the preface to the *Memoirs of Wolfe Tone*, written by his son in London, 1826:

> This wakening of the spirit of liberty roused from their long slumber of slavery the oppressed and degraded Catholics; who, by a strange anomaly, forming the original population of the country and the mass of people, were at that period, and are still in some respects, aliens in their native land. My father was the first Protestant who engaged in their cause to its whole length and experienced the greatest difficulty, in the beginning, to rouse them, if not to a sense of their wrongs, at least to the spirit of expressing them.

Constant propaganda also seeks to create the impression that it was the Protestant Scotch and Anglo-Irish who turned Ulster into a thriving province. Highly revealing on this score are the following passages from the preface to *An Historical Account of the Plantation of Ulster* by the Reverend George Hill, who was librarian at Queen's University, Belfast, from 1850 to 1880. This is still the definitive work on the subject, written by a Protestant clergyman of Anglo-Irish extraction:

> Among the descendants of the settlers it has been a cherished faith that our worthy ancestors came here to find homes only in a howling wilderness, or rather, perhaps, in a dreary and terrible region of muirland and morass. We very generally overlook the fact that the

shrewd and needy people whom we call our forefathers, and who dwelt north and south of the Tweed, would have had neither time nor inclination to look towards the shores of Ulster at all, had there been here no objects sufficiently attractive such as green fields, rich straths, beauteous valleys, and herds of Irish cattle adorning the hillsides. But such was indeed the simple truth.

The glowing account of Fermanagh, for example, from the facile and graphic pen of Sir John Davys, would have been at least equally, if not more appropriate as a description of Ulster in general; for although few of our northern counties are so picturesque as the one selected by him for special admiration, there are several more fertile and productive. "We have now," said he, when writing to Salisbury, finished [their work as plantation commissioners] in Fermanagh, which is so pleasant and fruitful a country, that if I should make a full description thereof it would rather be taken for a poetical fiction than for a true and serious narrative."

We are generally accustomed to believe that the Irish of Ulster, in the seventeenth century, were ignorant of all agricultural pursuits, including, of course, the management of domestic animals. Our plantation records, however, show us clearly enough we have been mistaken to a very considerable extent in this conclusion also. Their knowledge and management in such matters would fall far short, to be sure, of our present requirements; but, as compared with their neighbours, whether English or Scottish, it is pretty evident that the Irish of Ulster only wanted peace to enable them to excel both, as agriculturists.

During the seven years' war already referred to [the rising of the Northern chiefs under Hugh O'Neill] the native inhabitants of this province were reduced to the lowest depths of misery by the systematic destruction of their cattle and growing crops; but even in the brief lull or interval of peace that succeeded, from the spring of 1602 until the autumn of 1607, the recuperative process appears to have been of a very remarkable character indeed.

On the flight of the Earls at the latter date Sir Thomas Phillips made a journey from Coleraine to Dungannon, through the wooded country of Loch-inis O'Lynn, or Loughinsholin, and thereupon wrote to Salisbury, expressing among other matters, his unfeigned astonishment at the sight of so many cattle and such abundance of grain as he had observed all along his route from the one town to the other. . . . The hillsides were literally covered with cattle, where creaghting went on, no doubt in its most attractive forms; the valleys were clothed in the rich garniture of ripening barley and oats; whilst the woods swarmed with swine—20,000 of these animals being fattened yearly (as Phillips himself afterwards confirmed) in the forest of Glenconkeyne alone. . . . Sir Oliver St. John, who was intimately acquainted with the capabilities of the Ulster Irish as farmers, recommended that the escheated lands should be let directly from the crown to the natives who had been in possession, and who, in turn, would have given the king large rents.

All the windy rhetoric of a thousand Twelfth of July platform orations can't blow away these solid facts. What is so remarkable about this picture of Irish indestructibility of three centuries ago is that they had already passed through almost a thousand years of continual invasions, climaxed by an especially rough time during the regime of the Tudors.

One cruel distortion of the truth, designed to accentuate the religious cleavage in Ireland, centers around the figure of William of Orange. Of all the personalities in Irish history this monarch is without doubt the most misunderstood and misrepresented. Revered by the Irish Protestants, affectionately known in Ulster today as Prince Billy, his name the source for the Orange Lodge name, just as thoroughly hated by the Irish Roman Catholics, William was in fact progressive and liberal, free of all bigotry and sincere in his efforts to save the Irish from the fate mapped out for them by the English Parliament and people. He reinstated in his own handwriting the famous "omitted" clauses of the Treaty of Limerick, an action which would have prevented the seizure of over a million acres of land in Ireland if the English Parliament hadn't refused to ratify his signature.

Even more to the point as far as Irish bigotry is concerned, William was, in the broader European context, the most energetic member of the League of Augsburg, a firm friend and ally of Pope Innocent XII, the Holy Roman Emperor Leopold, as well as of the Roman Catholic King of Spain—the four of them united by their common enmity toward Louis XIV of France. After William's victory at the Boyne, Te Deums were sung in his honor and Masses celebrated in the Roman Catholic cathedral of Vienna, while Innocent himself was described as torn with conflicting emotions. Those Twelfth of July enthusiasts who scrawl on the walls of Belfast "Up Prince Billy! Down with the Pope!" should read a few unbiased history books, while those in high places on both sides, who should know better but seem perfectly content to let matters rest where they are, should take steps to dispel the unblissful ignorance of their respective flocks.

How the Irish Protestants were reduced to their present ineffectual status is a grim tragedy contained within a grimmer tragedy. It is a story that foreshadows many of the problems in the current Irish situation. From the early eighteenth century on it became apparent that England's quarrel with Ireland was not just one of religion. It embraced *everybody* who settled in Ireland.

After 1700, with the Catholics supposedly reduced to perpetual serfdom, the English opened fire on the newly arrived Irish Protestants, the very people they had planted in Ulster and other parts of the country. In a series of actions closely parallel to those directed against the thirteen colonies in America—and in many respects against Scotland and Wales—England succeeded in first crippling and finally destroying the new Protestant Irish nation. These actions lost England the American colonies. In Ireland they undermined the very cornerstone of the British Empire.

Exactly one century divided William Molyneux, the first Irish Protestant scholar to awaken to the dangers threatening his class in Ireland, from William Orr, the first Irish Protestant martyr to give his life for his country's liberty. In 1698 Molyneux published his *The Case of Ireland's Being Bound by Acts of Parliament in England*, in which he set forth the claim that England's power to bind the Irish by English laws was in itself illegal. The book was promptly burned by the common hangman, but a course was charted which Jonathan Swift and one or two others followed until finally the bulk of the Protestant Ascendancy in the 1760's realized Molyneux had been right all the time.

William Orr was hanged, drawn, and quartered in 1797 for administering the oath of the Society of United Irishmen, Wolfe Tone's organization. The society's motto was "Let the Nation Stand," its objective: "To obtain a complete reform of the legislature founded on the principles of civil, political, and religious liberty." Before his death Orr wrote: "All ground of jealousy between us and the Catholics is now done away with. They have denied us reform and them emancipation. They have oppressed them with penal laws and us with military ones. We are all subject to the tender, to dungeons, and to death. There is nothing surer than that Irishmen of every denomination must stand or fall together." Throughout the writings of Orr, Swift, Henry Grattan, and others one finds expressed the same broad principles which led to the creation of the new American nation.

The last golden opportunity for the Protestant Irish to work out peacefully their own relationship with England came and vanished during the eighteen years from 1782 to 1800, the years which marked the birth and untimely death of an independent Irish Parliament in Dublin. This was the brief period of glory for Georgian Ireland, transient glory reflected today in the exquisite architecture of town and country, in superb furniture, silver, book bindings, glass —and in little else. If the Parliament had been allowed to stand, a unified Ireland, far more capable of curing her own social ills, of settling her religious differences from within, would very likely have evolved into a close spiritual and physical alliance with England, much along the lines followed by the United States.

In her most colossal Irish blunder, however, England slaughtered the independent Parliament in 1801 by the so-called Act of Union. Two opportunities to rectify the situation did present themselves during the nineteenth century, the first under the leadership of Daniel O'Connell, the second under the closely coordinated joint leadership of Parnell and Prime Minister Gladstone, the *only* Englishman in a position of top authority during those bleak centuries who approached the Irish question on the grounds of Christian morality, of man's humanity toward his fellowman.

But one can scarcely classify these as golden opportunities. They were, at best, silver or bronze opportunities. After Parnell it became more and more apparent to clear-thinking people that Wolfe Tone had been right all the time, that Irish freedom could be won only by the same means with which it had been taken away—through the use of force.

The reasons England allowed an independent Parliament to come into being in the first place were essentially negative. At war with the American colonies and with France, threatened by this third potential adversary so close to home—an adversary deeply moved in spirit and intellect at its educated top level by what was taking place across the Atlantic—the British government under duress lifted one by one the restrictions imposed on Irish manufacturing and trade until by 1780 the underlying causes of friction between the Irish Protestant Ascendancy and the English Crown had been in large part removed. In the meantime during the latter half of the eighteenth century, the enforcement of the so-called penal laws had been gradually relaxed so that, while the condition of the common people was not materially improved, Roman Catholicism had been allowed to show its bruised and bloody head above water.

From 1800 on, the British government began to take full advantage of the religious cleavage in Ireland, a strategic "divide and rule" weapon which has been and still is wielded with consummate skill, first by Westminster, more recently and presently by Stormont. During the manipulations involved in the abolishment of the independent Irish Parliament, the Crown promised the Protestant Ascendancy they would staunchly support them on all fronts, while simultaneously the Irish hierarchy were assured they would be rewarded with immediate Catholic emancipation in return for their aid, two guarantees in direct conflict. It was not the last of double dealings.

The actual creation of the independent Irish Parliament in 1782 came about in an atmosphere reminiscent of Bunker Hill, Concord, and Lexington, under the pressure of the cannons and muskets of the brightly uniformed Irish volunteers commanded by the glamorous Napper Tandy. Most of the volunteers were Protestants. Drawn up in array outside the magnificent parliamentary building opposite Trinity College in Dublin, today the headquarters for the Bank of Ireland, they were ready to open fire with the weapons originally provided them by the British in the thought that they might help repel any invaders. The volunteers put across their argument. No "shot heard round the world" was fired. Parliament in England repealed Poynings's Law which dated back to Henry VII's time, and affirmed that "the right of Ireland to be governed only by the laws of the King and the Irish Parliament is hereby established forever, and at no time hereafter can it be questioned or questionable." In this case "forever" lasted for eighteen years.

The establishment of an independent Parliament in Dublin represented a vital point in Irish history which could have been, without bloodshed, comparable to the events involving force of arms that were taking place in America. But with the thirteen colonies irretrievably lost, with revolutionary France and in turn Napoleon ringing her around by a hostile alliance, England under the directorship of the iron-willed William Pitt began to call in the overdrafts that had been given to the Irish.

In the dissolution of the Irish Parliament and the passage of the Act of Union, a pathetic, hopeless chapter was enacted in the history of Anglo-Irish relationships which makes one stop and ask whether Christian white people in their dealings with one another—let alone with those of different creeds and colors—have added an ounce more of grandeur to the stature of the human race than they have detracted from it. In this scene all three major parties involved—the English, the Irish Protestant Ascendancy, and the Roman Catholic hierarchy—behaved equally disgracefully. Only the Irish people were absent.

As always, the voices of a small minority in England were raised in protest but to no avail. Charles

Fox summed up the feelings of Richard Brinsley Sheridan, Lord Cavendish, Lord Russell, Lord Fitzwilliam, and Lord Grey—all opposed to the Union—when he said, "We ought not to presume to legislate for a nation with whose feelings and affections, wants and interests, opinions and prejudices, we have no sympathy."

The execution proceeded, however, under the auspices of the Lord Lieutenant, Earl Cornwallis of Yorktown memory, and Lord Castlereagh, the Irish Chief Secretary, whose seat in the Irish Parliament had cost his father, Lord Londonderry, an estimated sixty thousand pounds in campaign expenses.

The Irish Protestant Ascendancy, which had bitterly fought off all attempts during the eighteen years of the independent Parliament to grant emancipation to the Catholics and to reform and broaden the legislature—although faced with a popular referendum of 700,000 signatures *against* the Union to only 6,000 in favor of it—succumbed to wholesale bribery, corruption, and royal baubles. In their own version of the "tennis court" oath, they blithely and permanently voted themselves out of office.

Twenty-two peers were elevated to higher rank, while twenty-eight gentlemen for the first time received titles, many of which still grace the Irish landscape. Others were rewarded with judgeships, pensions, loftier ecclesiastical assignments as in the case of the Protestant bishop of Cashel, while those in more stringent circumstances were given cold cash.

Henry Grattan, a Protestant who had courageously fought for the Catholics and who, though sick and old, tried unsuccessfully to stem the tide, estimated that only seven members who voted for the Union were *not* bribed. Of the three hundred members "one hundred and seventy two were absolutely the nominees either of the English government or of persons who held the power of nomination as their private property—in some instances, of English noblemen; in many instances, of absentee proprietors." Even a hardy campaigner like Cornwallis, sickened by what he saw, wrote to a friend:

> I long to kick those whom my public duty obliges me to court. My occupation obliges me to negotiate and job with the most corrupt people under heaven. I despise and hate myself every hour for engaging in such dirty work, and am supported only by the reflection that without a Union the British Empire must be dissolved.

Lord Castlereagh, described by Byron as "cold-blooded, smooth-faced, placid miscreant! Dabbling its sleek young hands in Erin's gore," recorded for a posterity that has forgotten all about it, the ignoble part in the deal played by the Roman Catholic hierarchy. In his memoirs he stated flatly that the Act of Union could never have been pushed through if the Irish Catholics had opposed it as a body. "The Catholic bishops were for the Union to a man, none so strongly as Dr. Troy, archbishop of Dublin."

Even though the rising of '98 had been put down, the wounded Wolfe Tone dead by his own hand, the northern Irish Protestant patriots—Henry Joy McCracken, Henry Monroe, the brothers John and Henry Sheares—all hanged, with Lord Edward Fitzgerald stabbed to death, and the two great priests who led the Wexford revolt obliterated—Father Michael Murphy killed in action and Father John Murphy hanged—the hierarchy, fluttering with nerves, was primarily concerned with the "forces of liberalism" abroad in the land.

In return for their invaluable aid, they got what they deserved, nothing of any real value. Pitt subsequently advised them with a long, sober face he was afraid to submit an Act of Emancipation to George III because, since the king had already been several times off his rocker, such a shock might well send him off again!

It so happened one of the most brilliant of all eighteenth-century English writers was in the Irish House of Parliament on the day the Act of Union was passed. Thomas De Quincey, then aged fifteen, had been visiting the young Lord Westport, son of the Earl of Altamont who voted for the Union and who in return was created the Marquis of Sligo. (His descendant, the present holder of the title, unlike most of those in similar situations, recently became an Irish citizen and works vigorously to improve conditions in his home county.) De Quincey, surveying the "whole assemblage of ermined peers" on that final day, reflected to himself:

> How is it, and by what unaccountable magic, that William Pitt can have prevailed on all these hereditary legislators and heads of patrician houses to renounce so easily, with nothing worth the name of a struggle, and no reward worth the name of an indemnification, the very brightest jewel in their coronets? This morning they all rose from their couches Peers of Parliament,

individual pillars of the realm, indispensable parties to every law that could pass. Tomorrow they will be nobody—men of straw—*terrae filii.* What madness has persuaded them to part with their birthright, and to cashier themselves and their children for ever into mere titular Lords? Observing a sarcastic smile on the lips of Castlereagh at the exact moment that the Bill was passed, "You are all," thought I to myself, "a pack of vagabonds henceforward, and interlopers, with actually no more right to be here than myself. I am an intruder, so are you."

Apparently they thought so themselves; for, soon after this solemn *fiat* of Jove had gone forth, their lordships, having no farther title to their robes (for which I could not help wishing that a party of Jewish old-clothesmen would have appeared and made a loud bidding), made what haste they could to lay them aside for ever. The House dispersed much more rapidly than it had assembled . . . and all parties adjourned to find what consolation they might get in the great evening event of dinner.

Thus ignominiously did the Irish Protestants as a *political governing party* comparable to the founders of the American Republic, throw away forever—or at least up until the present moment—the opportunity to lead the nation into the sunlight. From that time on dates their insignificant, generally negative role in Irish history *as a group or segment* of the population. It must be remembered, however, that *as individuals* a number of them continued to play gigantic roles in the struggle toward eventual, partial liberty and that, while there is a tendency on the part of a small-minded minority in the Republic to play down their accomplishments, without them and their inspiration, the Easter uprising in 1916 would never have taken place.

At the very moment when infamy was being enacted before Thomas De Quincey's eyes within the noble dimensions of the Dublin House of Parliament, most of the leaders dying on the battlefields, in prison cells, and at the end of the hangman's rope were Protestants who had despaired of gaining freedom by any other means than force. Except for Wexford where floggings, "half-hangings" on portable gallows, shootings, burnings, and other brutalities carried out mainly by Orange yeomanry, had goaded the peasantry into revolt, the Catholic populace remained generally quiescent, with such cities as Cork and Limerick, under the shepherding of local Catholic bishops, firm centers of loyalty to the British government, while Protestant Belfast and Dublin seethed with rebellion.

Nor should it be forgotten that Lord Edward Fitzgerald, younger son of the Duke of Leinster, one of the leaders killed in the 1798 rising, was a Protestant, as was Robert Emmet, who led almost single-handed his abortive uprising in 1803—a revolt which provided the basic plan followed during Easter Week. It was Emmet, before he was hanged and beheaded in Thomas Street, Dublin, who declared from the prisoner's dock, "When my country takes her place among the nations of the earth, then and not till then, let my epitaph be written." Since half-free is not free at all, it is appropriate that no one, Irish Protestant or Irish Catholic, has yet undertaken *this* writing assignment.

Outside of the political area Protestants continued to be in the vanguard of the national effort. The task of reviving the spirit and soul of the Irish was carried on in the nineteenth century primarily by the Young Irelanders—John Mitchel (whose grandson became mayor of New York City), John Dillon, Gavan Duffy, Thomas Davis (whose early death from scarletina robbed Ireland of her most promising son), Fintan Lalor, William Smith O'Brien, Thomas Francis Meagher (who later commanded the Irish Brigade in the Union Army during the American Civil War), and others who followed them. These men were about equally Catholics and Protestants. Working in close harmony, they were above all Irish Christian patriots who were never once wracked by sectarian interests.

First in *The Nation* and later in *The United Irishman* they linked together Ireland's ancient heritage with modern Irish history and in another direction identified Ireland's fight for freedom with comparable efforts in other countries. How badly the Irish need such a group of young men today! One contemporary English writer said of *The Nation*, "Ireland has at length, after weary and dumb ages of suffering and wrong, found a voice which speaks to some purpose. Five centuries of pain and injustice plead sternly and eloquently to God and man for redress." Comments P. S. O'Hegarty in his brilliant A *History of Ireland Under the Union*: "Young Ireland, which has dominated Irish political thought and political evolution ever since, first gave full and concrete expression to the Irish nation, neither Gale nor Seanghall, neither Catholic nor Protestant, but Irish. Henceforth, the Irish nation was out in the open."

While *The Nation* contained some of the finest Irish prose and poetry written in the nineteenth century, it was not a long-haired, intellectual project. It rapidly built up the largest weekly circulation in Ireland, was avidly read and discussed on remote farms and in distant villages. The Young Irelanders, breaking with Daniel O'Connell on the use of force—they were condemned by the Roman Catholic hierarchy as "atheists, anti-Catholics, Jacobins, and Separatists"—were the predecessors of those who carried on the great Celtic Revival at the turn of the century—Yeats, Douglas Hyde, and others—as well as the Fenians and those who rose up in arms in 1916.

Within themselves the Young Irelanders were a superb combination of men of action and men of thought, a breed of Irishmen which survived through Padraic Pearse, Thomas MacDonagh, Michael Collins, and their supporters but which seems, in terms of both Catholics and Protestants, totally absent from the Irish scene today. In the universality of their knowledge and the application of this knowlege to Irish affairs, they stand miles apart from the bulk of their present-day countrymen. Youthful Irish intellect and spirit appears to have gone down, down, down since 1922. Perhaps, as someone observed recently, all the "angry young Irishmen," in dismay and despair, are presently leaving the country rather than trying to solve its problems. As one concrete example, the late President Kennedy and his late brother Robert would have been very much at home among the Young Irelanders, whereas they would have been fish out of water in Ireland today.

The leavening of Catholics and Protestants was undoubtedly one of the prime reasons for the enormous impact the Young Irelanders had on their fellow countrymen. As one examines the modern scene in terms of the past, it becomes even more obvious that one of the problems, if not *the key problem*, facing the Irish today is how to get the Protestants back into the national picture where they belong.

While it looks like a gigantic assignment, opposed by many in high places, both Catholics and Protestants, it is by no means a hopeless situation. One of the most delightful aspects of the Irish is that the unexpected is always happening among them. Who knows what young Irishman, perhaps yet unborn, will lead his fellow Protestants back into the center of the national stage?

Over and above the still alive Protestant Ascendancy in Southern Ireland and the strangulating Orange/Union clique in the North, there is a third facet to present-day Anglo-Irish relationships which in the long run could prove the most disastrous of all to the Irish future. This is the extent to which the Republic's trade and finance are dominated by London. Over 70 percent of its exports went to Great Britain in 1967, and the percentage is growing. In 1966 a distinguished Oxford economist stated flatly that if the Irish, who should be experiencing a burgeoning economy, didn't quickly disentangle themselves from the current situation in Great Britain, "all the blood that flowed into the Liffey during the Troubles will have been shed in vain."

To explore the bewildering maze of these interlocking connections is something which will have to be left to the specialists. It is enough to say that while everything is being done to build up Irish commerce with the United States, with the Continent (as far as nonmembership in the Common Market allows), and with other parts of the world, Ireland is more dependent than ever, tradewise and financially, on the good will, good intentions, and prosperity of England. With the proper checks and balances, given Ireland's geographical location, this might be to a large extent as it should be. But on the basis of past performance and the present economic outlook in Great Britain, it is not what one would describe as an enviable position.

Leaving the English and Anglo-Irish out of the picture, and narrowing the focus down to the Irish Roman Catholic natives, it becomes all too obvious they are suffering from certain deep-seated maladies that can't be blamed on the presence of foreign bodies. Reviewing their history it seems fair to say that the Irish should, after half a century of independence, be doing a great deal better than they are. Until the Viking invasions in the late eighth century, a blending of Celts with an earlier stock created a civilization in Ireland which on a number of fronts reached heights unparalleled in Western Europe. For nine hundred more years, until the treaty of Limerick in 1691, the Irish, blended with some Danish and a great deal of Norman and old English blood, exhibited enormous powers of resistance and in the face of unceasing armed assault held together remarkably well as a nation.

During the seventeenth and eighteenth centuries those who with their traditional leaders fled the country wrote an astonishing historic chapter all across Europe and in the New World, a chapter which could only have been written by men of extraordinary physical and intellectual capacities. It is tempting to think that this siphoning off of youth, energy, and leadership resulted in the inadequacies which have prevailed ever since in the homeland—just as it is tempting to blame it on the Great Hunger, or on privation and oppression—but then one comes to the last incontrovertible fact, that those Irish who have accomplished so much abroad since the mid-nineteenth century, particularly in the United States but also in Canada, New Zealand, Australia, and England itself, sprang from this identical "depleted," "deprived," and "oppressed" stock.

After ten years I don't believe the Irish in Ireland are washed out or dried up as a nation. I have seen scores of young men in town and country who, if they were given the opportunity and the education, would match up on every count with Irish-Americans I have known well from coast to coast all across the United States, men who are running complex industries, occupying key executive positions, contributing in a major way to cultural, political, business, and civic activities. It is all one breed. The cleavage down the middle which took place among the Republican leaders in the twenties before the treaty with England was even signed has been pointed to by many as a vivid example of the classic inability of the Irish to work together as a nation. And yet, while the wounds were deep and are not completely healed, and while there are indications that a large percentage of the population is more locally oriented than nationally minded (which has its good as well as bad points), under the enigmatic, mystical father figure of Eamon de Valera, they have displayed, in spite of minor tempests in tiny teapots, consistent unity of purpose since the 1930's.

By a process of objective elimination, one is left with the other key element in the Irish picture which, in double harness with the English, emerges as the perennial, far more subtle villain of this piece, an element which today as never before exerts a permeating influence on all aspects of life in Ireland —the Roman Catholic *Church* as distinct from the Roman Catholic *religion.* At which point I hasten to add that, if the relationship between the hierarchy and the laity in Ireland were roughly comparable to what exists in the United States and in England today, this particular situation would be in large part swiftly corrected.

Those familiar with Irish history since 1800 know that the part played by the hierarchy in terms of *anti*-nationalism and *anti*patriotism, the ceaseless and bitter opposition to any attempts to change the status quo, to overthrow the forces of "law and order" as embodied in the British government, the violent antagonism shown toward the liberal, enlightened principles which did so much to release mankind in the Western world from servitude—at least the white portion of it—this entire disastrous, reactionary role has been touched on only lightly in these pages. The documentation is available for a major thesis and again one is referred to P. S. O'Hegarty's *Ireland Under the Union.*

Over and above the Church's opposition to the

Young Irelanders and its cooperation in helping to bring about the act of Union, are such revealing specifics as:

The letters of Wolfe Tone in which he expresses the vain hope that the clergy will remain neutral once the '98 rising begins. . . .

The group of self-aggrandizing Roman Catholics like Keogh and Sadlier who during the land wars of the nineteenth century were so noisily opposed to the aspirations of the native Irish under the leadership of the Protestant Charles Parnell and Michael Davitt they were unpopularly and widely referred to as "the Pope's Brass Band". . . .

The hierarchy's devastating role in the tragic fall of Parnell when they sealed his fate with the infamous Bishops' Manifesto of December 4, 1890, which stated in part that "without hesitation, or doubt, and in the plainest possible terms, we give it as our unanimous judgment that whoever else is fit to fill that highly responsible post [head of the Irish Parliamentary Party], Mr. Parnell decidedly is not". . . .

The autobiographies of such great Fenians as Jeremiah O'Donovan Rossa (*My Years in English Jails*), who set down in detail the shameful persecution and denial of the Sacraments suffered at the hands of the clergy from the day he started to fight actively for Irish independence. . . .

Down to the final upheaval in the twenties when the high churchmen who threw their weight and influence behind the rebellion could be counted on less than one full hand: Bishop O'Dwyer of Limerick —whose letters of 1916 to the British general, Sir John Grenfell "Bloody" Maxwell, are too long to include here—Bishop O'Hare in County Clare, and the expatriate Archbishop Mannix of Melbourne, Australia, who in 1920 was forcibly restrained from landing in Ireland and continued on to London where he officiated at the funeral of Terence MacSwiney, the lord mayor of Cork, whose hunger-strike martyrdom in Brixton jail had riveted the attention of the whole world on Ireland's predicament.

The only bellicose spirit exhibited by the hierarchy as a body, during the century and a half since 1829 when the churchmen got through Catholic emancipation what *they* were looking for, was when they engineered the formation of a voluntary Irish Brigade to fight on Franco's side in the Spanish Civil War.

In the aggregate, it is a sorry facet of the Irish story, one which has its roots deep in the past and which might best be forgotten if this same group, when the English were forced in 1922 to yield control to the Irish, hadn't eased themselves into the position of primary power, a position which they have steadily and stealthily strengthened each year up until the present.

One cannot be so naïve as to think that any power complex will react in the same way to conditions in all countries. The Communist approach to local affairs will alter drastically from one part of the world to another. Pope Paul recently assured a Yugoslavian delegation the last thing the Church wants to do is interfere in temporal affairs, but he must have been speaking of Yugoslavia, not Portugal, Spain, or Ireland. In Ireland, with the state abdicating its prerogatives and the people voiceless and defenseless, the Church, by persisting in what can only be described as a medieval, peasant attitude toward the Irish people, an attitude which appears to be designed *in toto* to keep conditions as they are, would seem to be storing trouble for itself. Especially since, with the world getting smaller via television and the jet planes, natives now have a chance to take a peep at what's going on elsewhere.

Specifically the hierarchy seems to be opposed to any sympathy and understanding between Irish Protestants and Irish Catholics, especially in terms of a united nation, to any raising of educational standards, to any real advances in social welfare and justice leading to higher standards of living, above all, to any assumption by the Irish individual of any self-authority and self-discipline.

What comes through instead is a fear on the part of the hierarchy that *any* change in Ireland will react against them. They have never had it so good, and they intend to keep it that way, giving just as little as possible as slowly as possible. Whoever tries to improve the situation in Ireland will do it not only without their help but, when the chips are down, in the face of their active opposition.

As a starting point it might be illuminating to present the Church's attitude toward the cleavage which exists between Irish Catholics and Protestants. If a young Catholic girl falls in love with a Protestant boy and goes to her parish priest for advice, she will be given any one of a number of pamphlets published by the Catholic Truth Society in Dublin. Most of them are highly personalized, highly dramatic tales featuring supposedly real-life people.

What is so distressing about these works is that

they confirm most of the charges leveled at the Roman Catholic Church in Ireland. They are addressed to an audience with the intellectual capacities and educational training of eight or nine year olds rather than young women of marriageable age. They are not what one would hope to find distributed to the members of a race with the literary and historic heritage of the Irish. They indicate a brainwashing which takes place from the cradle to the grave, which lays stress solely on the outward religious manifestations, and they reek with bitter hostility toward all other Christian sects, with the obvious purpose of engendering such hostility in the reader. Who can wonder on reading such literature why the ecumenical spirit has a sour breath in Ireland?

Running through all the tracts is the constant emphasis on the unimportance and triviality of this existence compared to the next one, a parallel line of thought to such past heresies as Gnosticism, Albigensianism, and Jansenism which more than any other factor in Ireland would appear to account for the paralysis and stultification of the Irish spirit. Joy is nowhere. Dread of hell and eternal damnation is everywhere.

One pamphlet sums up in succinct fashion the Church's attitude toward mixed Irish marriages:

> It is a recognized principle of right conduct that one may counsel evil when it is the *only alternative* to greater evil. One would seem to be justified in urging a broken-hearted husband to seek forgetfulness in drink rather than to persist in a purpose of committing suicide. . . . This is the sense in which the Church tolerates even those mixed marriages that are celebrated by

> dispensation. She is greatly pained by them. She is utterly disgusted by them. She is intensely disappointed by those who contract them. . . . She will have nothing whatever to do with the wedding unless the non-Catholic promises, in writing, to abstain from interfering with the Faith of the Catholic and to allow all the children, without exception, to be brought up as Catholics. But even when these promises have been made, it is only with tears in her eyes and a heart unable to be eloquent for mourning that the Church comes in the person of her priest to see one of her loved ones join in wedlock with a person who, consciously or unconsciously, is on the side of her enemies and playing false to the divine truth that is dearer to her than life itself.

And elsewhere:

> Like the good mother she is, the Church is nervous and unhappy when any of her children think to bind themselves in marriage to non-Catholics. She loves all men, even those who are most prejudiced against her, but she will not compromise with any evil or dangerous doctrines they may preach. Why blame her for loving her own deeply, and mother-like, for having a particular concern for their future? She sees clearly what foul thing heresy is, knows from long experience that it is an infectious disease, a cancer and sad blemish in the soul which has been purchased for the Spirit of Truth in the Blood of Jesus Christ; and so she will seek by all means in her power to discountenance mixed marriages, just as she will never repudiate the basic principle that a single human soul is a pearl above price, a gem far too precious ever to be risked, much less traded, for some few paltry years of earthly happiness. She is nothing if not faithful to the Truth.

Throughout, the inference is plain that any Roman Catholic who marries a Protestant is in grave danger of losing his or her immortal soul. The lines from William Drennan's poem in honor of William Orr, the first Irish Protestant martyr, return to mind:

*Hapless Nation! hapless Land!*
*Heap of uncementing sand!*
*Crumbled by a foreign weight:*
*And by worse, domestic hate.*

Besides these pamphets for those with special problems, a number of Irish newspapers feature daily or weekly columns written by members of the clergy, which hammer away along a dozen or so hard-and-fast narrow party lines. The columns are geared to a slightly higher audience level than the pamphlets. They are apparently directed toward those with the intellectual capacities of twelve to fourteen year olds. Radio-Television Erinn also carries a small number of "guidance and uplift" programs which feature members of the clergy but these, as well as Irish-language broadcasts, are luckily held down to a rational number by the fact that approximately half the residents of Ireland can switch over to either of two British channels.

It is impossible to estimate what the impact of television has been in Ireland. For the first time an iron curtain of strict censorship has been penetrated, and people who for generations dwelt in virtual isolation now hungrily view everything that can be seen. Television has provided a truly national medium of communication, which is bound to change the thinking patterns of thousands of individuals who spend their whole lives without moving outside a twenty-five-mile radius of their homes.

While there has been a good bit of talk about easing the censorship of books, foreign newspapers, magazines, and motion pictures, very little action has been taken. Much of the editorial material that appears in the London newspapers is deleted from Irish editions. Over ten thousand books have been censored since 1930. It is still against the law to buy or sell the major works of such writers as Thomas Wolfe, F. Scott Fitzgerald, Somerset Maugham, Graham Greene, Sinclair Lewis, C. P. Snow, William Faulkner, Alberto Moravia, Ernest Hemingway, Truman Capote, and André Malraux, to pull just a few names at random out of a huge pot. The average midwestern literary society in the United States would have to close its doors if it fell within the orbit of present-day Irish censorship. About half the motion pictures screened in England and America are banned, while others are cut indiscriminately before they are exposed to Irish eyes.

Many of the newspapers—Dublin dailies as well as sectional weeklies—perform another extremely valuable service designed to help the clergy keep the general public on their good behavior. Almost half of their news columns are regularly devoted to lengthy descriptions of venial sins and petty misdemeanors, primarily drunkenness and/or brawling charges, quarrels over land, traffic violations, complete with details of court proceedings, names and addresses of culprits involved. Nearly a century ago a French writer-traveler stated in wonderment that he had never seen any country with so little crime and so much crime reporting as Ireland. The practice has carried right through from days of servitude to days of freedom. Forty years ago most of the adolescents in Connecticut got their first inklings of sex via a Sunday newspaper which was widely distributed and exerted great political influence among the Roman Catholics in the state. It wasn't until coming to Ireland that I realized this since-abandoned U. S. journalistic venture was merely a carry-over from a standard, still-flourishing practice in the homeland of treating grown-up men and women like potentially naughty boys and girls.

In the average village and rural district, especially in the west, the parish priest occupies a position of unchallenged authority which extends over both education and spiritual guidance, as well as most social and community activities including charity benefits, annual fairs, dances, dramatic presentations, and sports. One rarely sees a news photograph of any local committee that does not include the parish priest among its members, and in the larger towns and cities there will usually be two or three men of the cloth included. A reviewer from one of the London Sunday newspapers who covered last year's Dublin Theater Festival devoted almost his entire column to the overwhelming impact both onstage and off of the ecclesiastical portion of the nation, of the intense preoccupation of Irish writers with religious matters. Rarely an evening passes without the television news broadcasts featuring one or more "events," the blessing of a new industrial plant, complete with holy water, the dedication of a new church, an item from the Vatican, a solemn requiem High Mass for an IRA hero attended by everyone from President de Valera down, the arrival or departure of some prominent member of the hierarchy at Dublin Airport.

Those Americans fortunate enough to have seen Brian Friel's *Philadelphia, Here I Come!* will have some concept of the intellectual and cultural blight which envelops the typical small Irish community and the extent to which this blight stems from the autonomy of the parish priests. Aside from the noncommunication between father and son, the most tragic aspect of this study in depth is the predicament of the young men, trapped within their village, fated to die without ever having really lived, captives of as ignorant a clergyman as ever strode onto the boards of a theater.

Having already seen the play in Dublin, I was particularly struck by the reactions of four Irish-Americans from New England, two married couples, who sat directly behind me at a performance in New York. They just couldn't believe this was a fair, unbiased presentation of contemporary village life in Ireland. Their protests became more and more audible, and they left in noisy disgust well before the final curtain, still cherishing their own private images which had nothing whatsoever to do with those of Brian Friel, a Roman Catholic Irish native.

Some parish priests are very popular. Others are heartily disliked. All of them are absolute monarchs in their own petty kingdoms, backed up when the going gets rough by extremely vocal episcopal support. During the past several years considerable newspaper space has been devoted to the urgent need for raising the standards of selection, training, and intellectual capacities—as well as the humanistic qualities—of the parish priests. Again, no concrete steps have been taken, or at least publicized. The more capable younger members of the clergy are in the main recruited for the numerous Irish missions which perform such tireless and splendid services across the face of the whole earth, and hardly a fortnight passes that a letter doesn't bring up in an editorial column the question whether some of this talent shouldn't be diverted to improving conditions at home.

At the time of his death, the energetic and broad-visioned Minister of Education, Donough O'Malley—supported in terms of moral and monetary aid by the equally energetic and broad-visioned Minister of Finance Charles Haughey—had been attempting to do, within the span of months, what should have been done during the past fifty years. He had been literally trying to lift the entire Irish educational system up by the bootstraps, starting with the primary schools, some of which he described as little better than "shacks and hovels," through a far broader participation in an improved and less expensive secondary-school system, to a university setup—spearheaded by his merger of University and Trinity colleges in Dublin—which in terms of physical equipment, curricula, faculties, and more enlightened intellectual climate could compete successfully with universities in England and other western European countries.

Despite minor snags, some rumblings and grumblings (until the recent merger it had been a mortal sin for Catholics to attend Trinity College without dispensations) Messers O'Malley and Haughey, backed by a few capable associates, had not encountered any serious opposition up until Mr. O'Malley's death. One can only speculate, however, especially with Mr. O'Malley gone, as to when and if the hierarchy will suddenly decide the state is invading an area which they have regarded for over three hundred years as their own private and semipublic bailiwick.

What is most distressing about village life in Ireland—a far drearier segment than either rural or urban extremes—is that there are few if any healthy social counterbalances to the influence and authority of the parish priest. There is, as mentioned before, no active, educated, coherent laity. The principal meeting ground, aside from the church, the school, and the hurling and football fields, is the pub. Even the smallest hamlet will usually have two or three of these, shoddy beyond description, where farmers and tradespeople will nurse for hours a bottle or two of stout while they mull over local affairs. Television has sharply cut down attendance but this medium can scarcely be classified as a communal activity.

Those who don't drink or can't afford to are seen standing at night in the shadows or under the infrequent arc lights along the main streets of the villages, their backs literally against the walls, in small groups or singly, observing what little of the world passes by. It is one of the most disturbing sights in Ireland. The absence of civic or recreational centers, of anything approximating a town hall, in most instances the lack of a public square or plaza, seem to be all part of a deliberate effort to keep communal affairs in the tight grip of the Church. The only other meeting places are the occasional dance halls and cinema houses which, like the pubs, are tawdry affairs and again under close clerical supervision.

One of the great shocks in Ireland is to find that a race of people capable of such glorious spoken and written artistry, surrounded by such incredible natural beauty, is devoid of any visual sense. This is reflected in all aspects of the man-made Irish scene—household furnishings which are ghastly, mass-produced paintings and sculpture which lean heavily toward religious subjects, clothes (the men appear to possess only two black suits, one for work, one to wear to church, with a choice of one or the other to be buried in), and above all, in architecture, both public and private. A high percentage of the total Irish village population has been transferred during the past twenty years from the ramshackle contiguous dwellings in or near the village centers—many of which have been left standing—to new, mostly gray or green, stuccoed council houses farther out from the centers. There is little to choose between the two types. It would almost seem that with imaginative renovating, plus proper sanitation and heating, much more could have been done with the original dwellings. Now and then one sees an exciting new school or church, but most are replicas of standard Victorian models or barrackslike "modern" buildings. The dreary pattern of the villages extends up through most of the larger towns both north and south of the Border. Some inhabitants strive manfully to improve the situation with brightly colored whitewash and gay flower beds, but the effect is somewhat comparable to hanging cheap jewelry on antiquated sluts.

One would like to invite the residents of about 85 percent of all Irish communities—excluding parts but not all of Dublin and Cork plus a handful of attractive villages—out on a picnic some sunny morning into the magnificent God-made, still largely unspoiled countryside, and while they were enjoying themselves, blow everything man-made since 1850 sky-high with dynamite, then level it flat to the earth so it couldn't be converted back into makeshift homes, stores, pubs, schools, and churches. At the same time all clothing except what was being worn, all surviving furnishings, all so-called decorative art, all knickknacks and gimcracks, would be piled onto mammoth bonfires. Starting from scratch, with most of everything pre-1850 as a nucleus, including ancient ruins and Georgian architecture, the Irish with a bit of planning couldn't possibly end up with anything as depressing and uninspiring as what they now have.

While these eyesores on the landscape are in part a heritage from the poverty-stricken past and have become more objectionable by being made of the cheap building materials common today in all countries, they also mirror the collective inner spirit of the modern Irish. The majority of the people, through long training, are so concerned with the ultimate destinies of their own souls that they just don't have the time or inclination to worry about what kind of physical surroundings they are going to bequeath to those who come after them. If you are living in a "vale of tears," if you are "poor banished children of Eve" inhabiting a "place of exile" which will soon be supplanted for all eternity by either heaven, hell, or purgatory, you can't afford to do more than tidy up a bit. Your descendants, if they are wise, will be equally worried about *their* ultimate destinations, so they won't care too much what sort of short-term accommodations are provided for them on earth.

The Irish attitude toward physical surroundings and the visual heritage passed on to succeeding generations reveals itself in a number of ways, some amusing, some highly disconcerting. In one of her books about Ireland, Kate O'Brien describes her astonishment at finding a farmer in the west who had planted *walnut trees.* Since walnut trees take about thirty years to grow to a reasonable height, here was one noteworthy exception to the general Irish rule, a man who was obviously attempting to do something about the milieu in which his children and grandchildren would live. In reverse, the common practice of not stripping ivy from trees both young and old throughout Ireland, particularly in the middle regions of the country, is rapidly creating a tree-stunted landscape which resembles photographs of French battlefields immediately after World War I. Widespread permanent damage is being done without a protesting voice.

Recently during a two and a half hour drive in a wide perimeter around London from Newmarket in Suffolk to Ascot in Berkshire, a careful check was made of the condition of the trees. Only three places were seen where ivy was in evidence. Driving the 120 miles across Ireland between Dublin and Limerick one finds only five or six places where the trees are *not* partially or totally destroyed by the same ubiquitous plant. Similar conditions prevail more or less everywhere.

The same lack of concern with how a place looks shows up in other ways throughout the rural areas, in overgrown, untrimmed hedgerows, mucky yards, makeshift fences and gates, claptrap hodgepodges of outbuildings. By contrast with the farms in France and Italy, owned in the main by fellow Roman Catholics, those in Ireland are a disgrace.

An underlying disinterest in the affairs of this world carries over into farming generally. No matter how small the acreage, Irish farmers prefer to raise cattle rather than till any sizable portion of the soil. It is not only easier, but it carries with it the ancient Celtic prestige associated with cattle raising. According to government land officials a great deal more could be done to improve what is passed on to the next generation, and there is practically no experimentation with different types of crops. Except for a few isolated instances, any attempts at cooperative farming have been discouraged by the clergy as smacking of socialism or communism, and the government has made no real effort to take the ball out of the Church's hands on this score. In the overall, it seems fair to say that about 25 percent of the farmers in the Republic are farming well, about 50 percent are farming in mediocre fashion, and the rest are doing a miserable job. Again the contrast with France and Italy is shocking.

All of this tends to bear out Bismarck's comment

that if you put the Dutch into Ireland they would turn hell into heaven and if you put the Irish into Holland, they would turn heaven into hell. Yet the descriptions quoted earlier of farming methods and farming results in Ulster during the seventeenth century—and there are others from elsewhere—prove that present conditions do not stem from any deep-seated, innate characteristics of the Irish. Rather they appear to be implanted characteristics.

If the clergy, who are desperately anxious to keep as many people as possible on the farms of Ireland, would for ten years omit all references from their pulpits and in the schools to this earth being a place of trivial, transient joys, a mere stepping-stone to celestial happiness, etc., and instead put positive emphasis on the obligations mankind has to those who come after them, on the joy of supplementing natural beauty with man-made beauty, on the need for devoting a reasonable amount of time each day to helping turn this world into a closer representation of the next one—in other words, if they would adopt an approach which is the direct antithesis of the present one—improvements could swiftly be made beyond all measure. The same change in philosophical emphasis would bear equal fruit in village, town, and city, would cause no loss of faith, and might well, more than any other single thing, help stem the disastrous tide of emigration which is agreed to be in large part due to psychological reasons.

Woven through the fabric of modern Irish life, scarcely indistinguishable from this disdain for all outward things of the earth, is a hidden, inner element, again ecclesiastical in origin, spotlighted by

Austin Clarke in his poem "The Straying Student"—the element he describes as having turned Ireland into a land "where every woman's son must carry his own coffin and believe, in dread, all that the clergy teach the young." By the time each Irish Roman Catholic, male or female, has learned to read or write, already deep within has been adroitly planted the sense of guilt for evil uncommitted, the guilt of original sin. By the age of eight or ten this guilt has become ingrained into the psyche, is there to be harped on continually as an unremitting chord throughout the rest of life.

It is a cancer that gnaws at the heart and the soul, breeds a disgust for the body, for one's self and one's shortcomings, that robs the individual of initiative and purpose. More than any other single factor it is the reason why, consciously or unconsciously, so many of the homeland Irish are immobilized as far as action is concerned. Such an approach to oneself and one's relationship to life and death threatens to turn, if it hasn't already done so, the native Irish from a race comparable to the ancient Irish into a permanent flock of terrified adult-adolescent zombies.

Only against the background of this kind of religious—one can hardly call it spiritual—training, is it possible to appreciate and understand the labyrinthine tortures of those who have tried to escape—such bedeviled figures as James Joyce, Samuel Beckett, Eugene O'Neill, Brendan Behan, and on a stage perhaps slightly more remote from the heart of the trouble, F. Scott Fitzgerald, John O'Hara, Edna O'Brien, James Farrell, and Mary McCarthy. The collective writhings and torments of such authors, all Irish by blood, all reared in various degrees of Irish Roman Catholicism, have contributed immensely to modern literature—in at least three cases on a gigantic scale—but the same anguish, bottled up within the Roman Catholic population of Ireland, incapable of self-expression, adds up to an overwhelming unseen but omnipresent state of national frustration and despair.

Those who never try to escape, who never seek to balance or rationalize their way of life or their philosophies, are not immune to torture. Many who never once waver in their faith still move through life in constant dread, not so much of death but of what may happen to them, or rather their immortal souls, after death.

Two of the most poignant remarks addressed to me in Ireland were made by the same prosperous, middle-aged man. He has been married for over thirty years, has four healthy children, is a devout Catholic who believes deeply and without question what he has been taught. To many it must seem as though he is enjoying a full, joyous existence. And yet his statements indicate the exact opposite.

The first time he said to me, "Do you know, my life has been one long duty. I've hated every minute of it. If I were given a choice, there's not one day I'd like to live over again."

The second time he said, "I hate my body. Everything about it. Sex. The daily functions. Everything. I hate being trapped in it. I wish I were a bird or an animal, with no consciousness of myself or what life is all about."

The roots of these remarks lie deep in an old-fashioned Irish Catholic training which is slowly vanishing from the American scene but is still the order of the day in Ireland, an early training which offers most people, whether they are aware of it or not, far more inner pain or torment than it does solace and support. Except perhaps as assuagement of that very pain and torment. This attitude toward daily existence is foreign to the average Italian or French Roman Catholic, and perhaps justifies the claim that Jansenism,* having been declared a heresy on the Continent, escaped via the back door into Ireland.

The essential quality of Irish Roman Catholicism and the dominant role the Church plays in politics, related affairs of state, and daily life, provide the Orangemen-cum-Unionists with practically their only, certainly their most eloquent, arguments against the reunion of the two severed parts of the country. During worldwide Ecumenical Week the single newsworthy event in Ireland took place when Roman Catholic Archbishop John C. McQuaid of Dublin issued a stiff-backed manifesto in which he declared that there is "only one true Church of Christ, the Catholic Church." Mr. Brian Faulkner, Northern Minister of Commerce, one of the most bombastic of the Orange Lodge spokesmen, seized the opportunity with obvious delight. It almost seemed as though the two of them must have discussed Ecumenical Week in advance on the telephone and worked out a "you say this, Mac, and I'll say that, Brian" routine, designed solely to drive their respective

* The doctrinal system of Cornelis Jansen and his followers, which denies free will and maintains that nature, including humanity, is fundamentally corrupt.

charges farther apart. It was a variation of the old one-two punch that has kept the Irish people groggy, bewildered, and disunited for almost two hundred years. "There is still in Northern Ireland mutual distrust," declared Mr. Faulkner, "and it is reawakened by such pronouncements as that of Archbishop McQuaid of Dublin."

Commenting on a sizable amount of publicity that followed the annual meeting of the Grand Orange Lodge, Mr. Faulkner continued:

> It is sometimes inferred that the members of the Order are retrogressive and not prepared to move with the new spirit of Ecumenism that is in the air. I believe this is untrue. I believe that the members of this institution will live up to the responsible position they hold in the country today, as they have done in the past.
>
> But as an organization dedicated to defend the principles of the Protestant faith, the Orange institution has also the responsibility of ensuring that in progressing toward a more liberal community we do not move too far, too fast. If the members of the Orange Order sometimes seem to move with caution, it is because they are afraid, however unfounded the fear may be, that cooperation is a one-way track.

The same warmed-over baloney. The same old hypocrisy and gross deceit. A curse on both houses. One would be inclined to put the Roman Catholic Seminary at Maynooth—popularly referred to as "the Irish White House" and in fact the center of hierarchical power—Stormont, and the headquarters of the Grand Orange Lodge at the very top of the "to be dynamited" list. What Mr. Faulkner chose to overlook was that Archbishop McQuaid's statement was greeted by a storm of protest throughout the Republic with only a few isolated voices raised in his defense. Many of the most vehement objections came from Roman Catholic student and other fledgling lay organizations. The very fact the archbishop had chosen Ecumenical Week made a special mockery of his pronouncement.

Out of centuries of persecution and bigotry directed against them the Irish Catholic people have learned if no other lesson that of tolerance. Unlike most puritans they are too preoccupied with their own sins to worry about those of others. The status of the Protestant Ascendancy within the Republic is sufficient case in point.

It seems inconceivable that the general public of Ireland—Protestants and Catholics alike—especially the young Irish, will allow themselves to be led down the garden path much longer, that unlike the citizens of some nations, unlike the Young Irelanders before them, they will fail to see that their strength lies only in unity. Yet in spite of the great past leaders of both sects who have pointed the way to the light, the picture as of now is a discouraging one.

While the problems of the Irish by comparison with other parts of the world may appear mundane, two fundamental, inescapable truths emerge which have universal, timeless application:

First, that the attempt on the part of one group of people to enslave and hold in subjugation another group of people can only in the end lead to misery and disaster for both.

Secondly, if Christians of the same color and essential blood can share the same tiny island for so many hundreds of years and still get on so badly together, how much more understanding and patience is going to be required in other parts of the world where there are far more serious differences of color, creed, and political philosophies?

It is worth asking Arabs and Jews, Indians and Pakistanis, Cypriots, Rhodesians, South Africans, North and South Koreans, North and South Vietnamese, Americans of both continents, people everywhere, to reflect for a brief moment on the unfolding tapestry of the Irish tragedy, a tragedy that has not yet run its course. May they then go and do otherwise to one another.

As for the homeland, until Irish Protestants North and South put their nation above narrow, partisan interests, until the English wake up to the fact that in spite of the past a united Ireland can be their strongest ally and friend, until the heads of state in the Republic, as the heads of state in other Roman Catholic countries have had to do, push the Church out of affairs in which it has no business, and until the hierarchy releases the Irish Catholics from the medieval spiritual dungeon in which they have been imprisoned for so many years—until then one can only mutter under one's breath, with mixed feelings of hope and despair, "God save Ireland!"

The events which landed the Irish in their present unenviable situation are veiled in obscurity and ignorance, have been muddied up with half-truths, deliberate lies, and distortions. Anglo-Saxon scholars have twisted key facts, blurred and suppressed others to fit their own concept of what happened, have often stoutly and successfully maintained the Irish have no history at all.

Irish scholars, when not accepting this simplified version, have been faced at almost every stage of the past with embarrassing facts which fail to dovetail with the "official" versions, have fogged and stereotyped their conclusions to a point where they bear as little relationship to the truth as the Anglo-Saxon presentations. One can piece together out of brilliant individual studies a story which has significance in terms of the present, but these studies are buried under an avalanche of dull, standardized mishmash. Even such a painstaking work as Cecil Woodham-Smith's *The Great Hunger* is already being chipped away at by less painful, less accusative, watered-down pamphlets, lectures, and books explaining what "really" happened during those crucial mid-nineteenth-century years.

Most of the problems faced by the Irish today stem from the sixteenth century. Until then the Irish nation, having reached its essential, permanent form —a blend of pre-Celt, Celt, Dane, Norman, and Old English—could have moved in any one of a number of directions. During that century the fatal die was cast. After the battle of Kinsale in 1601 relationships between Ireland and England were set squarely on a downhill track that was bound to lead to disaster. The miracle is that any of the native Irish who remained in Ireland during the past three hundred years survived.

During the sixteenth century, the English managed to drive the three major segments of the Irish—the common people, their leaders, and the Anglo-Norman/Old English element (the English already settled in Ireland)—irrevocably into the arms of Rome, arms which the English themselves had only abandoned in 1534 under the leadership of Henry VIII. By doing this the English lost to Rome the "spiritual" victory over the Irish which finally in 1922 cost them the shaky and constantly threatened "physical" domination they enjoyed after Kinsale.

Roman Catholicism became inseparable from Irish nationalism, just as Protestantism became an integral part of nationalism in England. The English took possession of the "body" of Ireland. The Church of Rome took possession of the "soul" of Ireland. So it has remained for better or worse ever since. In one of the most pertinent comments ever made on the Irish dilemma, George Bernard Shaw wrote at the turn of the century in his "Preface for Politicians" to *John Bull's Other Island*:

> In Ireland England is nothing but the Pope's policeman. . .. The British government and the Vatican may differ very much as to whose subject the Irishman is to be; but they are quite agreed as to the propriety of his being a subject.

Despite the existence of a "free" Republic today—through on one hand the Protestant Ascendancy in the South, the Orange Order in the North, and England's domination of Irish finance and trade, and on the other the assumption of increased temporal powers by the Church—this same team of two essentially *foreign* power complexes still cheats the great bulk of the Irish people out of their rightful heritage.

On the surface, especially in view of the deep-rooted sectarian animosities still rampant in Ireland, it seems remarkable that the inhabitants of Great Britain, who for almost a thousand years had been allied with Rome, ended up Protestants in the sixteenth century, while the Irish with fiercely independent religious traditions landed en masse in the Roman Catholic camp. The biggest single lie told to the Irish people is that their ancestors were in the *Roman* Catholic Church ever since the days of St. Patrick and/or St. Peter, depending on which facet of the lie is to be emphasized. The truth is that it wasn't until the sixteenth century, a thousand years and more after those two early saints had departed from the temporal scene that, as the English abandoned the Roman Church, the Irish took their place within the fold. (Those seeking more information on the subject should read Robert Dudley Edwards' superb study, *Church and State in Tudor Ireland.*)

Originally Henry VIII, after breaking with Rome, embarked on a course of moderation and conciliation with the Irish chiefs which, if it had been followed for a century, might well have created a climate of mutual prosperity and harmony into which religious changes and compromises could have been gradually introduced.

Judging from state papers which date back to 1520 a policy of conciliation was the one that had always appealed most to the Tudor monarch, whereas his Irish council strongly recommended a plantation of the entire island by English settlers. At the Dublin Parliament of 1541, which proclaimed Henry King of Ireland, more than forty of the most powerful Irish chiefs submitted to him. These submissions entailed a direct repudiation of the Pope and an agreement "to resist any attempt at papal jurisdiction" within their lands. Among those who submitted and signed the repudiation were the O'Briens, the Burkes, the Fitzpatricks, the O'Neills, the O'Donnells, the Fitzgeralds, the MacCarthys, the O'Sullivans, the O'Mores, the O'Connors, the Barrys, the Roches, the MacMahons, and the O'Rourkes—about an equal number stemming from Norman and native Irish origins.

Many of the leaders also accepted English titles, assuming a status comparable to the already knighted

Earl of Desmond (Fitzgerald) and Earl of Ormond (Butler). The O'Neill became the Earl of Tyrone, Ulick Burke the Earl of Clanrickarde, Fitzpatrick the Baron of Upper Ossory, while the O'Briens assumed two peerages, the earldom of Thomond and the barony of Inchquin. Numerous lesser titles were accepted, including three by the O'Donnells, who under James I were elevated to the earldom of Tirconnell. MacCarthy Môr was shortly after created the Earl of Clancarthy and declared that he intended to have the oath of supremacy sworn to by "all the members of his state."

While this political program was under way, certain developments on the religious front grievously and permanently damaged the English cause and Protestantism among both the Anglo-Norman/Old English segment and the native Irish people, as distinct from their chiefs. The former group who should have been counted on as loyal subjects of the Crown were put on the horns of an unsolvable dilemma by the act which proclaimed Henry "the Supreme Head on Earth of the Church of England and Ireland." Since the time of Henry II and the first Norman invasions of Ireland, the English in Ireland had been under the joint protection of King *and* Pope. The Church of Rome had always stood behind them, ready if necessary to invoke the weapon of excommunication against any rebellious Irish enemies.

Even more important it was only through the Pope, through the controversial bull of Adrian IV, that the King of England had any lawful claim to his temporal lordship of Ireland which he occupied in vassalage to the Pope, a subordinate position which prompted

Henry to assume the kingship of Ireland, the first English monarch to do so. The lands, the privileges, the legal rights of Henry's subjects within the Pale and in the fortified seaports rested firmly on the doctrine of papal supremacy which Henry was mercilessly attacking. A blow aimed at the Pope was a blow aimed at the cornerstone of the traditional English position in Ireland, something which seems odd today.

Two statements most pertinent to the past and current state of affairs in Ireland were made by the same leading Roman Catholic churchman in the first half of the nineteenth century. At the beginning of the fight for Catholic emancipation J. W. Doyle, bishop of Kildare and Leighlin, proclaimed for all to hear, "If a rebellion were raging from Carrickfergus to Cape Clear, no sentence of excommunication would ever be fulminated by a Catholic prelate." Near the end of the fight—with the populace wildly excited and convinced that Daniel O'Connell was about to direct his fire toward repeal of the Union with England or was even prepared to lead them out in armed rebellion—one finds the same man, Bishop Doyle, delivering the following remarkable oration before an English House of Commons committee on the state of Ireland:

> I am fully convinced that if the disabilities under which the Roman Catholics labour were removed we would be so incorporated by interest and affection with the State that the same pledge which is required of his Majesty's other subjects—namely the oath of allegiance—would be sufficient to secure our attachment at all times to the Crown and to the institutions of the coun-

> try; for our religion, our Church rather, is in its nature monarchial. It has, I might say, a natural tendency to support a Kingly government, and if it were to do anything to disturb or destroy the institutions existing in these countries, it would be acting as it were contrary to its own nature. . . . We have no mind, and no thought, and no will, but that which would lead us to incorporate ourselves fully and essentially with this great Kingdom, for it would be our greatest pride to share in the glories and riches of England.

So there it was out in the open, 655 years after Strongbow's landing at Waterford, the same basic singleness of purpose uniting the English Crown and the Church of Rome in common action against the Irish people, here reaffirmed by the official mouthpiece of the Irish hierarchy—the same old party line which contributed to some of the most frightful disasters in the past and which, unless the reunification of Ireland evolves peacefully, will assuredly lead to major catastrophe in the future.

Of special interest is the careful distinction Bishop Doyle made between "our *religion*" and "our *Church*." While no one would wish to deny that the Roman Catholic religion has been the chief—at times the only—solace and support of the Irish people, no such position of honor can be set aside for the Roman Catholic Church. In a paraphrase to the old adage that marriage is an institution designed to help two people endure problems that wouldn't exist if they weren't married, one might say that the Roman Catholic *religion* has helped the Irish people endure problems, many of which wouldn't have existed if it hadn't been for the Roman Catholic *Church*. Daniel O'Connell struck at the same nail from a different direction when he said, "We'll take our religion from Rome, our politics from home," an adage which, alas, he and others often forgot, and many are still forgetting.

While a considerable amount of Irish land passed into English hands during the first half of the sixteenth century, once Elizabeth ascended the throne, the pace quickened, reaching a level comparable to the conquistadores' excursions into Mexico and Peru which were taking place during the same uncomfortable century. The similarities are striking, since in each case long-established peoples with highly developed cultures, customs, and traditions were overwhelmed from outside by a new species of adventurer and buccaneer, ruthless in search of wealth and power, playing according to gangster rules that were strange to their victims.

In each case, even though in Ireland white Christians were pitted against white Christians, religion provided a handy pretext for masking the predatory intentions of the attacking parties, at the same time moving some elements to fanatical extremes. On both sides of the Atlantic one witnessed situations in which rooted *minorities* were dispossessed, persecuted, and in the end reduced to serfdom by foreign *minorities*, a process which was later repeated in Africa.

The total amount of land stolen in Ireland during the sixteenth century, by comparison with what happened in the seventeenth century, was chicken feed—half a million acres in Munster and a million and a half acres throughout the rest of the country. But it was a fair start and whetted the appetites of those who came after. The entire story of how property in Ireland was lifted out of Irish hands by the English—the Irish ended up in 1700 with about 5 percent of the arable land—is one that cries for a specialized study comparable to *The Great Hunger*.

After Henry VIII's break with Rome, the mass of the Irish people, like their leaders, showed little interest in the technical question of papal supremacy. The first Jesuit mission to Ireland in 1541 and the first visit by a legate from the Vatican aroused no widespread enthusiasm.

Only by a series of actions that indicate an appalling ignorance of the true state of affairs in Ireland did the Crown create an entirely new set of conditions which forever after, in the average Irish mind, associated the English no longer with Roman Catholicism but with Protestantism—a jointly detested association which in itself was enough to drive the native population into opposition. Some of these actions struck at superstitions and customs which predated Christian belief and practice, the two often deeply entwined with one another.

Under Dr. George Browne, an English Augustinian who was consecrated archbishop of Dublin without the sanction of Rome, a loudly publicized campaign was launched by the Crown to remove and destroy certain relics and images that had been venerated since time immemorial by the Irish population. It was also announced that the ancient custom of pilgrimages to holy sites, which again dated back to pagan times, was to be banned.

The first three places to be stripped of images and

relics, with wooden tables substituted for the traditional stone altars, were the national shrine of the Blessed Virgin at Trim and the two oldest churches in Dublin—St. Patrick's Cathedral and Christ Church which had been founded by the Danes. The whole country was horrified to hear that the Baculum Jesu, the supposed staff of Christ which had served as St. Patrick's crozier, had been publicly burned by Browne in Dublin. Some thirty more churches, chapels, and shrines were despoiled in the Pale, Tipperary, Galway, and as political domination was extended, in Cork and other parts of the country. Shortly after, the attorney general and solicitor general, again with a fanfare of publicity, journeyed to the great place of worship at Cashel. Their trumpeted intentions were to stamp out "idolatry, papistry, the Mass Sacrament and the like." Thus the Crown neatly, if a bit undiplomatically, linked the Pope to the very things the Irish cherished most in life. Out of such actions sprang the discord that has persisted ever since.

Even more disastrous to the English cause was the wholesale destruction throughout Ireland of friaries, abbeys, and monasteries whose ruins today dot the countryside. Included in the burning and looting were Clonmacnoise and other early centers of learning and faith. Not only were the people horrified by these desecrations, as they had been centuries earlier during the Viking invasions, but hordes of mendicant monks and friars, especially members of the Franciscan order, were turned loose, homeless and without pensions, among the people. They were soon moving about from village to village, preaching against "despoilers and heretics," at the same time providing the only available spiritual nourishment, since nothing of any significance was done by the English government in Irish areas to substitute new clergymen or places of worship.

Sharing the privations and sufferings of the populace, closely united to them by the bond of language, these simple priests forged a relationship which firmly withstood all subsequent reforming efforts. In fact, so closely identified became the cause of the priests with the cause of the people, that in later centuries a high percentage of the descendants of Cromwellian settlers and other English planters eventually made their way into the ranks of the Roman Catholics. At the same time these friars and monks, cut off from England, formed or strengthened ties directly with their parent orders on the Continent; as the century progressed they found their way back and forth more and more to Rome, their missions becoming increasingly political as well as spiritual. Many of them were executed without trial, each death widening the chasm between the Crown and the Irish people.

To make matters worse, the destroyed monastic centers had in most cases served as the only schools, hospitals, and homes for travelers, as well as dispensing charity among the poor. While it was occasionally suggested by government officials that money from the confiscated Church lands be earmarked for these purposes, nothing was ever done. It was also decreed that no burials could be made within these former sites, and since in many instances these had been the only cemeteries, the people were faced with a choice of breaking the law or burying their parents, children, and relatives in unconsecrated ground.

Above everything else, the English government seemed to be totally unaware that the Irish spoke Irish not English, that it was asking a good bit of their own clergy to convert an alien people to a particular way of spiritual life when they didn't have the faintest idea what was being said to them. (Even the chiefs who submitted to Henry in 1541 had to have the chancellor's speech translated into Irish by the Earl of Ormond.) As part of the monarch's determination to anglicize the Irish, it was decreed that the Mass should be said in English, and three years later an order went out that "every curate was to teach the Pater Noster and Creed in *the mother tongue—English*"! Although frequent suggestions were made on the subject it was not until the reign of James I in the next century that the English Book of Common Prayer and the Reformed version of the Bible were translated into Irish. By then the people had long since made their decision as to where they would seek spiritual sustenance. The struggle for the soul of Ireland was over and won by Rome before the English woke up to the fact that it had begun.

There is an illuminating, firsthand description from the seventeenth century which, even more than the picture of farming conditions in Ulster during the same period, gives one cause to ruminate on the *inherent* characteristics of the Irish as compared to those *implanted* during recent drab decades. Dionysius Massari, dean of Fermo, secretary to Archbishop Rinuccini, papal nuncio to Ireland, wrote in Italian from Limerick in 1645, a few years prior to Cromwell's descent on Ireland, to Rinuccini's brother in Florence:

The men are fine-looking and of incredible strength, swift runners, and ready to bear every kind of hardship with cheerfulness. They are all trained in arms, especially now that they are at war. Those who apply themselves to letters are very learned, and well fitted to the professions and sciences.

The women are distinguished by their grace and beauty, and they are as modest as they are lovely. Their manners are marked by their extreme simplicity, and they mix freely in conversation on all occasions without suspicion or jealousy. Their dress differs from ours, and is somewhat like the French. They also wear cloaks reaching to their heels and tufted locks of hair, and they go without any head-dress, content with linen bands bound up in the Greek fashion, which display their natural beauty to much advantage. Their families are very large. Some have as many as thirty children, all living; not a few have fifteen or twenty, and all these children are handsome, tall and strong, the majority being fair-haired, white-skinned and red-complexioned.

Food is abundant, and the inhabitants eat and entertain very well. They are constantly pledging healths, the usual drinks being Spanish wines, French claret, very good beer and excellent milk. Butter is used abundantly with all kinds of food. . . . There is also plenty of fruit —apples, pears, plums and artichokes. All eatables are cheap. A fat ox costs sixteen shillings, a sheep fifteen pence, a pair of capons, or fowls, five pence; eggs a farthing each, and other things in proportion. A good-sized fish costs a penny, and they don't worry about selling game. They kill birds almost with sticks. Both salt and fresh water fish are cheap, abundant, and of excellent flavour. . . . The horses are numerous, strong, well-built, and swift. For five pounds you can buy a nag which in Italy could not be got for a hundred gold pieces.

Some idea of the devastation wrought in the mid-seventeenth century by Cromwell can be gained by the following well-known description of Ireland written only ten years after Massari's letter. It is from J. P. Prendergast's *The Cromwellian Settlement of Ireland*:

> Ireland, in the language of Scripture, lay void as a wilderness. Five-sixths of the people had disappeared. Women and children were found daily perishing in ditches, starved. The bodies of many wandering orphans, whose fathers had been killed or exiled, and whose mothers had died of famine, were preyed upon by wolves. In the years 1652 and 1653 the plague, following the desolating wars, had swept away whole counties, so that one might travel twenty or thirty miles and not see a living creature. Man, beast and bird were all dead or had quit those desolate places.

British authorities estimated that before 1641 there were six Irish people to every English person in Ireland and that by 1655 three fourths of the land and five sixths of the houses were in the possession of English settlers. Not only the native Irish but Normans, Anglo-Normans, Old English—Roman Catholics and Anglicans alike—had been forced by law off their holdings, either into exile or west of the Shannon. Sir William Petty fifteen years later made a survey for the English government which revealed that three quarters of the Irish population lived in cabins without chimneys or windows, subsisting mainly on potatoes and a little milk.

The treaty of Limerick in 1691, the greatest single swindle in Irish history, climaxed a century of land-grabbing which put Queen Elizabeth and Bloody Mary to shame. By 1641 the Ulster Plantation, inaugurated by Ireland's supposed Stuart friend, James I, had transferred 3 million of the 6.5 million acres in six counties—Donegal, Derry, Tyrone, Fermanagh, Cavan, and Armagh—into Scottish and English hands. Between 1610 and 1625 further plantations were established in North Wexford, South Carlow, Longford, Leitrim, and South Offaly, all of which became in 1641 flaming centers of rebellion.

F. J. C. Hearnshaw, late Emeritus Professor of History at the University of London, who could hardly be described as partial to the Irish, paints in one sentence a striking picture of conditions in Ireland when James I died in 1625 and Charles I ascended the throne: "Every Irish landlord was trembling for the security of his title, dreading the pernicious activity of the discoverers, and of the lawyers that followed them as jackals follow tigers."

One of James I's last acts was to set up a Defective Titles Commission which was to "discover" legal flaws in Irish titles, confiscate the lands in favor of the Crown, which in turn would grant them to new settlers. Under Charles I this commission in 1625 took over major portions of Sligo, Mayo, and Galway in Connacht, Clare and Tipperary in Munster, and large tracts of additional land in Leinster. It seems unbelievable that the Irish people were tricked into giving up their own fight for freedom in order to try to put this monarch back on the throne of England.

It seems equally unbelievable that today, with the last three of the Stuarts—the Old Pretender, Bonnie Prince Charlie, and Henry, Cardinal of York, Charles' brother—buried in the crypt of St. Peter's at Rome, this family is held up for constant veneration in Irish textbooks and in a constant flood of laudatory literature as staunch supporters of Ireland and her people. It is only one of a dozen ways, involving the past and the present, through which the Irish, for reasons they will apparently never understand, are kept in a state of ignorance.

It also focuses the spotlight on the most important question of all: "How can the English and the Irish, the Catholics and the Protestants, ever become true friends until they learn how they turned into such bitter enemies?"

What happened to the terms of the treaty of Limerick in 1691 set the stage for the final degradation of the Irish people. Conditions arose which still affect the present situation in Ireland. The ink had hardly dried on the treaty when a large French fleet carrying a powerful force of seasoned veterans sailed up the Shannon, but Patrick Sarsfield refused to renege on his word. If he could have foreseen how the terms of the treaty were to be carried out, he would undoubtedly have picked up his sword and plunged back into action. Certainly he and his followers would never have left Ireland.

On paper the thirteen civil articles appeared more than generous. They guaranteed among other things that the Irish fighting men and their families would not be deprived of their property, a simple oath of allegiance to William and Mary would be substituted in place of the hated oath of supremacy, the Catholic religion would not be banned in Ireland, nor would anyone be persecuted for his faith.

It was also agreed that the fourteen thousand Irish fighting men still under arms would be given a choice of either sailing for France or, after taking an oath of allegiance, returning home or enlisting in the British Army. Of this force, representing the essential vitality and youth of Ireland, over twelve thousand with practically every one of their traditional leaders, elected to go to France where they felt they could best continue the struggle for freedom. They were hardly on their way down the Shannon before chicanery began.

The Penal Laws enacted shortly after the treaty provided that Irish Catholics were forbidden to practice their religion, to vote, or to engage in trade. They were forbidden to live within five miles of a corporate town, to hold public office, to own a horse worth more than five pounds. They were forbidden to carry arms, to enter a profession, to purchase land, to receive a gift of land or any inheritance from a Protestant. They were forbidden to rent any land worth more than thirty shillings a year, forbidden to educate their children at home or abroad or send them to a Catholic teacher. No children could be left under Catholic guardianship on the death of the parents; if a son or daughter turned Protestant, all property went to that person. During the early part of the century quite a large number of Roman Catholics whose descendants are still in Ireland turned Protestant to recover their lands. Even those who didn't turn were ordered to attend Protestant services which was enforced by law until 1869.

Roman Catholic priests were outlawed, and for a time there was a bounty of five pounds for the "head of a priest, a teacher, or a wolf." While there were slight relaxations as the century proceeded, with Mass being said in the open air or in out-of-the-way chapels and with "schools" being conducted behind hedges or in ditches, one finds as late as 1776 Lord Charlemont, after introducing a bill into the Irish Parliament that allowed Catholics to lease a cabin and a potato garden, being physically manhandled and hustled out of the chair.

What little is known about Roman Catholic life and living conditions in eighteenth-century Ireland is gained mainly from the writings of the English, the Anglo-Irish, and a few travelers from other lands, most of whom recoiled in horror from what they saw. Whereas even in the seventeenth century, which could hardly be described as a cozy bed of roses, the people are often described as full of gaiety and a zest for life, after 1700 the picture is one of unending dreariness, oppression, privation, apathy, and despair. A few excerpts will suffice:

Jonathan Swift, a Protestant who became the intellect and voice of "savage indignation" for all of Ireland, Protestants, and Catholics alike, wrote of

> . . . the miserable dress, and diet, and dwelling of the people. The general desolation in most parts of the Kingdom. The old seats of the nobility and gentry all in ruins, and no new ones in their stead. The families of farmers who pay great rents, living in filth and nastiness upon butter-milk and potatoes, without a shoe or stocking to their feet, or a house so convenient as an English hog-sty to receive them.

Bishop Berkeley, also Protestant, asked in his famous *The Querist*, published in the 1730's, among other unanswered questions, "Whether there be upon earth any Christian or civilized people so beggarly, wretched, and destitute as the common *Irish?*" Commenting on the huge supplies of beef, pork, and butter being shipped out of Cork in a single year, and of the wool and leather being exported, Berkeley asked: "Whether a foreigner could imagine that one-half of the people were starving in a country which sent out such plenty of provisions?" "Whether she would not be a very vile matron, and justly thought either mad or foolish, that would give away the necessaries of life, from her naked and famished children, in exchange for pearls to stick in her hair and sweet meats to stick in her palate?" This was the identical situation a hundred years later when the Great Hunger began. Plentiful shipments flowed steadily out of Ireland each year during the potato blight while a million people starved to death and several million more fled the country.

The most famous firsthand detailed picture of the Irish common people as they were in the eighteenth century appeared in Arthur Young's *A Tour in Ireland*, published at London in 1780 as part of a series describing conditions in various countries. This Englishman, again a Protestant, covered both the psychological and the physical aspects of what was happening in Ireland:

> The landlord of an Irish estate, inhabited by Roman Catholicks, is a sort of despot who yields obedience, in whatever concerns the poor, to no law but that of his own will. . . . A long series of oppressions, aided by many very ill-judged laws, have brought landlords into a habit of exerting a very lofty superiority, and their vassals into that of an almost unlimited submission: speaking a language that is despised, professing a re-

ligion that is abhorred, and being disarmed, the poor find themselves in many cases slaves even in the bosom of *written* liberty. . . .

A landlord in Ireland can scarcely invent an order which a servant, Labourer or cottar dares to refuse to execute. Nothing satisfies him but an unlimited submission. Disrespect or anything tending towards sauciness he may punish with his cane or his horsewhip with the most perfect security; a poor man would have his bones broke if he offered to lift his hand in his own defense. Knocking down is spoken of in the country in a manner that makes an Englishman stare. It must strike the most careless traveller to see whole strings of cars whipt into a ditch by a gentleman's footman, to make way for his carriage; if they are overturned or broken in pieces, no matter, it is taken in patience; were they to complain they would perhaps be horsewhipped.

The cottages of the Irish, which are all called cabbins, are the most miserable looking hovels that can well be conceived: they generally consist of only one room: mud kneaded with straw is the common material of the walls; these are rarely above seven feet high, and not always above five or six; they are about two feet thick, and have only a door, which lets in light instead of a window, and should let the smoak out instead of a chimney, but they had rather keep it in . . . the smoak warms them, but certainly is as injurious to their eyes as it is to the complexions of the women, which in general in the cabbins of Ireland has a near resemblance to that of a smoaked ham. . . . The furniture of the cabbins is as bad as the architecture; in very many consisting only of a pot for boiling their potatoes, a bit of a table, and one or two broken stools; beds are not found universally, the family lying on straw. . . .

The roofs of the cabbins are rafters, raised from the tops of the mud walls, and the covering varies; some

> are thatched with straw, potato stalks, or with heath, others only covered with sods of turf cut from a grass field; and I have seen several that were partly composed of all three; the bad repair these roofs are kept in, a hole in the thatch being often mended with turf, and weeds spouting from every part, gives them the appearance of a weedy dunghill, especially when the cabbin is not built with regular walls, but supported on one, or perhaps on both sides by the banks of a broad dry ditch, the roof then seems a hillock, upon which perhaps the pig grazes. . . .

A particularly edifying episode was described by Edward Wakefield, an English Protestant who undertook a tour of Ireland at the suggestion of Lord Oriel, speaker of the Irish Parliament:

> The poor are much neglected by the richer class in this district; and I have seen some glaring instances of the tyranny and oppression to which they are subjected: I shall mention one. In the month of June, 1809, at the races of Carlow, I saw a poor man's cheek laid open by a stroke of a whip. He was standing in the midst of a crowd, near the winning post: the inhuman wretch who inflicted the wound, was a gentleman of some rank in the county, but his name for many reasons, I shall not mention. The unhappy sufferer was standing in his way, and without requesting him to move, he struck him with less ceremony than an English squire would a dog. But what astonished me even more than the deed, and which shows the difference between English and Irish feeling, was, that not a murmur was heard, nor hand raised in disapprobation, but the surrounding spectators, dispersed, running different ways, like slaves terrified at the rod of their despot.

Balancing off these vignettes of Georgian country life in Ireland, Lord Nuneham reported in his *Harcourt Papers* (1772) on the prevailing climate in Dublin:

> The pageantry of the procession to the House of Lords and the homage paid to the Lord Lieutenant did not enchant me; for it exceeded even what I had expected; and the grenadiers on horseback, the principal officers of the household with their wands, and the pages in their liveries, paddling on foot through the mud, with grooms of chambers and footmen, through the streets lined with soldiers, had an air of absolute monarchy and of military force to support it, that had I been an Irishman I could not endure the sight of.

It is only when viewed against such a background that the position of the Protestant Ascendancy in Ireland today comes into proper perspective.

Now, as often happens, when the British government had effectively crushed the Irish Protestants as a political governing body by ending the independent Parliament in Dublin and forcing through the Act of Union between England and Ireland, quite a different situation developed than the Crown had anticipated.

The great nameless mass of Roman Catholics began to surge back up into view. The whole period of Irish history from 1800 to the present represents a series of writhings and twistings on the part of the Irish people to burst out of the chains of bondage, an effort which only partially succeeded in 1922.

Some idea of the indestructible nature of the Irish people can be gained from the fact that from 1700 to

1800 the total population, in spite of the numbers who fled or were transported overseas, increased from 1.5 million to over 4 million, and by the 1840's when the potato blight struck, it had reached 8.5 million, about one third that of England, over double what it is today. The most revealing picture of conditions *prior to the hunger years* is found in a single sentence written by the Frenchman Gustave de Beaumont who came to Ireland after having studied firsthand slavery in the American South. De Beaumont stated that the Irish peasants were worse off than the Negroes, sunk to "the very extreme of human wretchedness."

A few glimpses will suffice to show those who have not read *The Great Hunger* what happened in Ireland during the 1840's. The great Irish Protestant writer and patriot, John Mitchel, later deported for life, traveled across the country from Dublin to Galway and reported:

> We saw sights that will never wholly leave the eyes that beheld them, cowering wretches, almost naked in the savage weather, prowling in turnip fields, and endeavouring to grub up roots which had been left, but running to hide as the mail coach rolled by; groups and families sitting or wandering on the high-road, with failing steps, and dim, patient eyes, gazing hopelessly into infinite darkness and despair; parties of tall, brawny men, once the flower of Meath and Galway, stalking by with a fierce and vacant scowl, as if they realized that all this ought not to be, but knew not who to blame, saw none whom they could rend in their wrath. Sometimes I could see, in front of the cottages, little children leaning against a fence when the sun shone out—for they could not stand—their limbs fleshless, their bodies half-naked, their faces bloated yet wrinkled, and of a

pale, greenish hue—children who would never, it was too plain, grow up to be men and women.

N. M. Cummins, a justice of the peace in Cork, described in a letter to the Duke of Wellington, dated December 17, 1846, a visit he made to an apparently deserted hamlet near Skibbereen in a lovely stretch of West Cork country. Entering the first hovel, he found that

> . . . six famished and ghastly skeletons, to all appearance dead, were huddled in a corner on some filthy straw, their sole covering what seemed a ragged horse-cloth, and their wretched legs hanging about, naked above the knees. I approached in horror, and found by a low moaning they were alive, *they were in fever*—four children, a woman, and what had once been a man. It is impossible to go through the details, suffice it to say, that in a few minutes I was surrounded by at least 200 of such phantoms, such frightful spectres as no words can describe. By far the greater number were delirious, either from famine or from fever. Their demoniac yells are still ringing in my ears, and their horrible images are fixed upon my brain. My heart sickens at the recital, but I must go on. In another case—decency would forbid what follows, but it must be told—my clothes were nearly torn off in my endeavours to escape from the throng of pestilence around, when my neck-cloth was seized from behind by a grip which compelled me to turn. I found myself grasped by a woman with an infant, *just born*, in her arms, and the remains of a filthy sack across her loins—the sole covering of herself and babe. The same morning the police opened a house on the adjoining lands, which was observed shut for many days, and two frozen corpses were found lying upon the mud floor, *half devoured by the rats.*

Justice Cummins ended his letter to Wellington, "Once more, my Lord Duke, in the name of starving thousands, I implore you break the frigid and flimsy chain of official etiquette, and save the land of your birth—the kindred of that gallant Irish blood which you have so often seen lavished to support the honour of the British name—and let there be inscribed upon your tomb, *Servata Hibernia.*" Needless to say, such inscription is absent from said tomb.

When one stops to think how many personal counterparts to descriptions like the above have been handed down by word of mouth from grandparents to parents to children to grandchildren in villages throughout Ireland, it is understandable why so many of the Irish today look on the Border and Partition not so much as a new glorious experiment in good neighborliness but as the final degrading tail twisting to centuries of tyranny, privation, and blatant mismanagement. These firsthand reports from the 1840's bring home much more vividly what happened than does the round figure of a million people starved to death in Ireland during five or six years. A considerable number also died before they ever reached the Promised Land across the Atlantic. Exactly how many nobody knows. Records show what happened in 1847 on certain of the so-called coffin ships—108 people out of 440 died on the *Larch,* 137 out of 493 on the *Queen,* 236 out of 552 on the *Avon,* 267 out of 476 on the *Virginius.* Because of pestilence many were not allowed to come ashore on the mainland but were herded onto coastal islands where a large percentage died and were buried in trenches.

The flight of the Irish from Ireland didn't end with

the end of the hunger years. It stepped up in tempo during the decades that followed until out of more than eight million people only half remained. And so the population figure has stayed ever since.

And yet it was out of the depleted ranks of these people that the leaders of the 1916 Easter uprising sprang unheralded and almost unknown. With revolver and rifle, machine gun, bomb, and bayonet, they underscored at the General Post Office in Dublin with their own blood the words of Parnell inscribed on his monument farther up O'Connell Street: "No man has a right to set bounds to the march of a nation."

They were a pathetically small handful, those leaders, and completely out of step with the vast majority of their fellow countrymen. They were laughed and sneered at by the Dubliners when they were herded through the streets to jail and execution after the rising failed. Their armed followers were never numerous, even at the height of the subsequent Troubles, at most seventeen hundred men under arms at any one time. Yet through martyrdom and unflinching courage and persistence they slowly won the support of the Irish people and eventually their partial freedom.

One might almost believe Arthur O'Shaughnessey was being prophetic when he wrote forty years earlier:

*One man with a dream, at pleasure,*
*Shall go forth and conquer a crown;*
*And three with a new song's measure*
*Can trample an empire down.*

During the past few years I have come to know extremely well ten or twelve young men who are close neighbors in the Limerick farm country where we live. I have been with them day after day and watched them at work, both in outside occupations and doing two major jobs of construction, first converting outbuildings into a small factory and later restoring a house after a bad fire.

They are everything that the Anglo-Irish say they are not: conscientious, hardworking, intelligent, full of good spirits, uncomplaining, in every way capable of forging a new nation. And yet, given the present set of conditions in Ireland, hamstrung as they are by the same old team of the British and the Roman Catholic Church, they have no more chance of bettering their lot than if they were among the Eskimos.

I have seen where and how these young men, their brothers and sisters and their parents live, or rather subsist. I have talked with enough of them long enough to know their quiet resentment at what fate has laid out for them on this planet, and have sensed their inability to escape from destiny—or to create a new destiny—except by fleeing from their mother country.

I can only assure you again: After nearly half a century the bulk of the Irish in Ireland still live in physical and spiritual servitude. Those whom they looked on as their jailers have long since departed from the Republic. The prison doors are unlocked and stand open. But the Irish loiter in their cells, staring at the sunshine streaming through the bars and in at the doors, afraid to go outside.

Three years ago I had the good fortune to dine with the late Donough O'Malley, his wife, son, and daughter in the roof-garden restaurant of the Hilton Hotel in Rome. At that time he was Minister for Health, forty-four years old, brimming with energy, confidence, and enthusiasm. Looking out across the gaily illuminated shadows of the Eternal City, he sketched with intense, unbottled emotion the seemingly eternal plight of the people in his own native city of Limerick and on the farms in the surrounding countryside. He talked of the destitution and neglect of the old people, of the slum conditions still prevailing, of the urgent need for higher health, recreational, and educational standards among the young people.

It was not that things were any worse in Limerick City and County than elsewhere. He just happened to know that particular situation best from long, firsthand experience. This was where his enormous voting strength lay, among the poor common people of his constituency and it was they who, turning out literally by the thousands, almost swamped the politicians and the clergy at his funeral.

O'Malley that summer in Rome was readying a broadly based bill designed to attack some of the more pressing social-welfare problems. It was legislation described in his obituaries as obviously heading for stiff opposition from "the doctors and bishops," and a month or two later, before the bill was submitted, his party leader, Mr. Sean Lemass, suddenly yanked him out of the Health Ministry assignment. It was more than apparent there was no desire in high places to have this brilliant, impetuous fledgling, a special favorite of President de Valera's, ground up into small pieces by the same hierarchical forces who in 1951 all but wrecked the equally promising career of Dr. Noel Browne who today as a leader of the Labour Party lingers on like an accusing ghost at a banquet but who at the time was Minister for Health in a coalition government under de Valera.

Dr. Browne had been busily and openly engaged in preparing what is still referred to as the Mother and Child Bill which would have extended free hospital care to a large portion of the needy in Ireland. Without warning he not only ran head-on into an ecclesiastical concrete wall but in an all-night session his fellow cabinet members voted one by one not to support him.

It was a highly dramatic episode which pointed up two basic truths in modern Ireland: First, just because they are rarely pushed into a position where they have to exhibit their collective power does not mean that the hierarchy isn't perpetually on guard against any real or imagined infringements of what they have marked out as their own domain. And secondly, there are few if any politicians in Ireland who would dare by word and/or deed to attempt to clarify in the minds of the devout voting public the essential differences between a *religion* and a *Church.* At least not *their* religion and *their* Church. The politicians, in short, from the very top to the bottom, are running scared of hierarchical power. And they have good reason to be.

With the spearhead in the assault on the antiquated citadel of Irish education shattered by death, it seems scarcely likely O'Malley's program will take form as his memorial. While he sounded a courageous battle cry when, with the merger of Trinity College, the bastion of Irish Protestantism, and University College, Dublin, he announced that he had "neither sought nor obtained the approval of the hierarchy," while his charm beguiled the clergy as well as the laity, even if he had lived the path ahead would have been strewn with rocks and full of pitfalls.

In spite of the rugged persistence and far-ranging intellect of Mr. Haughey, the Minister for Finance, the experience of Dr. Michael Hillery, Minister for Labour—who as a former Minister for Education broke ground for Mr. O'Malley with his plea "Give every child a chance!"—and the talents of the genial Mr. Brian Lenihan, who has succeeded O'Malley as Minister for Education, at this writing the citadel looks unconquerable. Even the merger of Trinity and University College has bogged down. And without a massive effort on the educational front one can whistle in the wind for any really worthwhile long-term advances in Ireland.

When one looks at O'Malley's background it is surprising that, unlike the vast majority of well-off twentieth-century Irishmen, Roman Catholic or otherwise, he was imbued with such radiant social consciousness. Like James Joyce he was a product of Clongowes Wood College, the most celebrated institution of the Jesuits in Ireland. Clongowes Wood can best be termed an Anglo-Saxon Roman Catholic stronghold, the emphasis on such alien sports as rugby and cricket with a curriculum devoid of national spirit.

Joyce reflected this outlook in the feelings expressed about his fellow Irishmen, notably in *Dubliners* and *Ulysses.* Leaving Ireland before the Easter uprising, he missed the awakening experienced by Yeats, failed to realize that within the shoddy characters he depicted with such acid satire were qualities of nobility and grandeur.

Nowhere is there a more devastating summing up of the intellectual and spiritual accouterments of the twentieth-century Irishman—as conceived by Joyce—than in the scene from *Ulysses* which takes place in Barney Kernan's pub when he describes, among mock epic passages which would almost put one off Irish mythology forever, "The Citizen" seated at the bar, the last of the heroes, his walking stick propped up beside him, his mongrel dog Garryowen slumbering noisily on the floor, while the master waits patiently for someone to buy him a drink. "From his girdle hung a row of seastones which dangled at every movement of his portentous frame and on these were graven with rude yet striking art the tribal images of many Irish heroes and heroines of antiquity," at which point Joyce unreels a staggering list of several hundred names, ranging through CúChulainn, Patrick Sarsfield, Red Hugh O'Donnell, Goliath, Henry Joy Mc-

Cracken, the Village Blacksmith, the Man that Broke the Bank at Monte Carlo, St. Brendan, Marshal MacMahon, John L. Sullivan, Sir Thomas Lipton, Patrick W. Shakespeare, Brian Confucuis, Murtagh Gutenberg, Patricio Velasquez, Boss Croker, Thomas Cook and Son, Jeremiah O'Donovan Rossa, the Lily of Killarney, etc. etc. etc. etc. etc. It is a monumental heap of ridicule, yet out from under the heap crawled handfuls of men just like "The Citizen" who set Dublin on fire in 1916.

The impressions of Clongowes Wood College contained in *Ulysses* and *A Portrait of the Artist as a Young Man* have been analyzed and reanalyzed but far more pertinent as to what is wrong with the average "educated" modern Irishman—and what made Donough O'Malley's presence on the contemporary Irish scene even more remarkable—was the career of a lesser-known contemporary of Joyce's at Clongowes Wood.

Michael Joseph Rahilly, known as The O'Rahilly, was the *only* wealthy, landed Roman Catholic who led and was killed in the Easter uprising. He was shot down directing an attack against a British barricade in Moore Street a block from the General Post Office, on Friday evening of Easter Week. He had counseled against taking up arms, but when the die was cast, he explained in a note, "If the men I have trained to fight are going into action, then I must be with them."

In a biography, *The O'Rahilly*, Marcus Bourke in 1967 traced the unexpected development of this Clongowes Wood student into a dedicated patriot and martyr. Bourke speaks of the college as having been a "bulwark of West-British Ireland" where The O'Rahilly learned "practically nothing about his native country. . . . England remained the spiritual home of those who directed the affairs of the Jesuit society in this country [Ireland]. . . . Irish history or literature found no place in the curriculum of Clongowes." As in *A Portrait of the Artist as a Young Man,* which Bourke quotes, "the boys were divided, for the purpose of rivalry at arithmetic, into York and Lancaster." And "Irish games were then never seen on the playing fields of Clongowes; then as now rugby was the principal game of the college. To this day Clongowes regards itself as the nursery of Irish cricket; in O'Rahilly's time it used the game as an excuse to entertain Her Majesty's officers from the nearby Curragh camp." Clongowes was not "prepared for rebels."

On the positive side, Bourke attributes the awakening of a nationalist sense in The O'Rahilly to his delving into regional history and archaeology. On the negative side, "his distaste for the way of life of upper-class loyalist Dublin" which he was exposed to during the first four or five years of marriage was responsible for "his final conversion to what was then known in polite circles as advanced nationalism." In the first of many letters which appeared in the *United Irishman,* starting about ten years after he emerged from under the wing of the Jesuits, The O'Rahilly signed himself "A Clongowes Boy." The letter, headed "West Britonism," accused Father James Daly, prefect of studies, immortalized by Joyce in *A Portrait* as "Father Dolan" with the "cruel no-coloured eyes," of attempting "to sap the national spirit" of his charges. In other letters The O'Rahilly directed his scathing ridicule against the Roman Catholic upper class in Dublin who sought to emulate and fawn on the Protestant Ascendancy and Crown officials.

What is of course most significant about The O'Rahilly is that in his views he was virtually unique among his own class. While things may have improved somewhat at Clongowes Wood College, one fact is certain: The overwhelming majority of wealthy Irish Roman Catholics today are ultraconservative in their political, economic, and social principles. They stand at the opposite pole from The O'Rahilly. Many of them privately believe it was a great mistake ever to have broken off from England, and an equal number want no trouble over Partition—in fact a high percentage are frightened to death of the competition to their own businesses from the North which would result if the country were reunited. The same thing applies to the Common Market. Some of the most vehement attacks have come from prominent businessmen.

Those in the United States familiar with the Roman Catholic splinter group within the Democratic Party which under the leadership of Al Smith, John J. Raskob, and others broke with Franklin D. Roosevelt over what they considered his "socialistic/communistic" program—not to mention those who realize how many wealthy Irish-American Roman Catholics have been bitterly opposed to the Kennedys and all they represent—will not be surprised to learn that their counterparts in Ireland stand a good deal farther to the right of center. They are not by half ready to see the national budget spent on long-term schemes to raise educational, health, and general living standards.

When one considers the scarcity of such figures as The O'Rahilly and Donough O'Malley in twentieth-century Ireland, it would appear highly desirable to ship several hundred promising young men out of the country each year for a less fettered, more intensive training abroad, young Irishmen who might later return to bring this training to bear against homeland problems. Even *twenty* men a year (*so trained*) would help. It is pathetic to see the Irish trying to improve conditions in Katanga, Cyprus, Yemen, Vietnam, and other trouble spots without ever coming to grips with their own predicament.

Completely dominating the Ireland of this century are two personalities who will assuredly command more and more attention from historians and dramatists in the years ahead. On the one side is Eamon de Valera, today in his eighties, almost totally blind, a legend in his own lifetime, the only truly potent force in the Republic aside from the hierarchy, for while he has long since turned over the reins of power to the clergy, he has regularly and adroitly blocked anyone else from making proper use of temporal authority.

On the other side looms the gigantic, veiled spirit of Michael Collins, the leader of the year-old Irish Free State, killed in a West Cork ambush by an assailant's bullet forty-six years ago. His memory is as cherished in Ireland today as when he died.

Eight years ago, like most Irish-Americans I regarded de Valera as the greatest of living Irishmen, one of the immortals. During the time spent in Ireland I have slowly and reluctantly come around to the view held by many objective people that while he has undoubtedly provided a rallying point for the Irish, he is one of the greatest disasters ever inflicted on the nation. In spite of the official and semiofficial smoke screen of laudatory propaganda that envelops him in his Phoenix Park mansion, in spite of the praise that will unquestionably be heaped upon him when he passes to his reward, the documentation of cold facts already put together indicates that history will not treat him kindly.

To state it briefly and bluntly—the Irish heroes who won freedom in the twenties entrusted the jailers' keys to de Valera, and he promptly handed them over to the hierarchy.

Like many others I find myself brooding over what might have happened if Michael Collins had survived the twenties and Eamon de Valera had disappeared from the scene. Along with the Protestant Ascendancy, the Orangemen of the North, the English government, the hierarchy, and the upper-class Roman Catholics, de Valera—who never successfully coped with these forces—unfortunately and unwittingly has earned a place among them as one of the lids that for nearly fifty years has been securely screwed down on the heads of the Irish people.

One would like to skirt around or brush lightly over this central figure, but the influence of de Valera on the entire course of modern Irish events is too widespread for him to be avoided. In many respects the honorary President of Ireland arrived where he did through the elimination of other extremely promising young leaders and one can hardly reach any other conclusion than that some of the most crucial eliminations stemmed directly or indirectly from de Valera himself.

One is faced with a career the early stages of which consisted primarily of a ruthless, skillfully executed campaign for personal power, which involved along the way excommunication and savage condemnation by the Roman Catholic Church. The second half, stretching out from the time in 1927 when he finally grasped the power he had sought, looks suspiciously like a colossal act of atonement, played against a national backdrop, with the protagonist increasingly surrounded and counseled by the same clerical characters who so recently had censured him. The unfortunate thing is that the Irish people have had to do penance, have had to endure a half century of purgatory, along with the repentant sinner.

Michael Collins and Eamon de Valera first appeared together on the same page of history during Easter Week, 1916. Collins, a new recruit to the volunteers, fresh from employment with the Guaranty Trust Company in London, was not important enough for the English to kill after the rising failed. Little realizing he would become their most dreaded adversary, they interned him along with most of the survivors in Frongoch Camp, Wales. De Valera's sentence of death was commited to life imprisonment because, having been born in New York, he possessed an American passport. He too was interned.

The wave of horror which swept Ireland at the news of the executions of many of the rebel leaders and the callous manner in which they were carried out not only more than any other single thing cost the English eventual possession of Ireland but redounded very much to de Valera's favor as one of the few top survivors. The intense emotion of the people fastened eagerly upon him.

During the fourteen months the rebels were interned, details of the executions, which were dragged out from May 3 to May 16, were widely circulated throughout Ireland. All those who had signed the proclamation of the Irish Republic were shot dead, as well as eight others active in the fighting. Joseph Plunkett, who would not have lived long, having been just operated on for glandular tuberculosis, added pathos to an already melancholy situation when he married, a few hours before he faced the British rifles, his fiancée, Grace Gifford, in the chapel of Kilmainham Gaol. (Later it was claimed that Irish Roman Catholic members were among those at Westminster who applauded when his execution was announced.) The bridal couple were wed by the light of a candle held by an English soldier, the prison lighting system having failed.

The circumstances surrounding the killing of the last man, the Labour Party leader James Connolly, aroused far and away the most universal revulsion. According to Father Aloysius, who was with Connolly until the end, "They carried him from his bed in an ambulance stretcher down to a waiting ambulance and drove him to Kilmainham Gaol. They carried him from the ambulance to the gaolyard and put him in a chair . . . and then they shot him." He was put into the chair because, being weak from wounds in his legs and in great pain, he was unable to stand up. From then on the British general who ordered the executions was known among the Irish as "Bloody" Maxwell. Within a few months an ordinarily docile, peace-loving populace was temporarily roused to a feverish pitch of patriotism.

It is said that de Valera himself was stunned by the reception given him when he returned to Ireland at the head of the freed rebels in June, 1917. Unlike the exuberant, gay-spirited, handsome Collins he was in appearance not an heroic figure. According to Terence de Vere White, literary editor of *The Irish Times,* in his superb biography of Kevin O'Higgins, there is no evidence de Valera ever squeezed the trigger of a gun during the Easter uprising, the Troubles, or the Civil War, and these statements have never been officially contradicted. He was, most dangerous of all, a man of indirect action. In 1917 he looked more like a schoolteacher than a popular leader—tall, gangling, bespectacled. Although a difficulty in pronouncing his *th's* apparently created a certain remoteness from the crowds, his impassioned speeches rapidly increased his popularity. He won a by-election that summer in East Clare and at the Sinn Féin Convention in October was unanimously elected president of the party and shortly after president of the Irish Volunteers.

The roles of Collins and de Valera during the years that followed, up to the proposed signing of the treaty with England, have been charted out in minute detail by such uncommitted writers as Frank O'Connor, de Vere White, P. S. O'Hegarty, Clifford King, Max Caulfield, Rex Taylor, Edgar Holt, and a number of others. *Not one of them* plumps down on the side of de Valera. De Valera had and still has passionate admirers, authorized biographers and apologists, and he occupies an unshakable position in the hearts of thousands of simple Irish people; no one can question his intense patriotism, but the overwhelming weight of detached opinion is that he not only did far less than Collins to set Ireland free, but in his growing jealousy of and animosity toward "the Big Fellow"—a petty animosity shared and fanned by his two chief lieutenants, Cathal Brugha and Austin Stack, who ended up losing their lives in de Valera's behalf—by his haggling opposition to Collins over the treaty and his refusal to accept its ratification first by the Dáil (the Irish assembly), and later by the Irish people, which in turn plunged the country into bloody civil war and brought about the murders of Collins, O'Higgins, and others of both factions, he did immeasurably more harm than good in terms of the future of the Irish nation.

Up until the treaty, while Collins, who was a perfectly balanced combination of action and thought, concentrated all his energies toward winning the war—directing the fighting, the intelligence operation and the financing—de Valera spent most of his time outside the country. Although he did invaluable work enlisting support for the Irish cause in America, a great deal of time was devoted to advancing his own personal cause. There are elements in the situation reminiscent of the parallel careers in Russia at that same time of Trotsky and Stalin.

The stage of de Valera's career which has caused and will continue to cause the most problems for his admirers is the period following the ratification of the treaty in the Dáil on January 7, 1922, by a vote of sixty-four to fifty-seven and the subsequent rejection of de Valera as President of the Republic in the same body by a vote of sixty to fifty-eight. This must have been a particularly cruel blow, but he was in essence making the preposterous suggestion that he should take over control of a government which had voted contrary to him on the only burning issue of the moment.

With a general election coming up in which the question of the treaty was to be taken to the people, de Valera headed for the speaking platforms. If on any occasion during this junket he had focused attention on the implications of Partition, there would have been an excellent, tangible reason for what he did. It was the only portion of the treaty of any deep significance, yet neither he nor anyone in either faction was apparently awake to this for many months to come. Reading back through the transcripts of Dáil proceedings, one finds hair-splitting distinctions involving various forms of association with England and oaths of allegiance, but never once was the question of Partition seriously debated. There are vague attempts today to create the impression that de Valera was anti-treaty because of Partition, but the records emphatically deny this.

What de Valera did do was go out and in inflammatory terms urge his listeners, with special attention directed toward the younger men, to continue the fight for Irish freedom. On March 16 he first made it clear that in his mind civil war was inevitable: "If you don't fight today, you will have to fight tomorrow; and I say, when you are in a good fighting position, then fight on."

The next day in County Tipperary, before a St. Patrick's Day crowd that included scores of IRA men, he declared that instead of fighting foreign soldiers, it would perhaps now be necessary for the Irish people to fight the Irish troops of an Irish government set up by Irishmen. That unless the treaty were rejected, it might be over the bodies of the young men he saw around him that the fight would be continued. In the same county that day others heard him repeat that, if the treaty were accepted, the work of the Volunteers during the past four years would have to be completed, not over the bodies of foreign soldiers, but over the bodies of their fellow countrymen. They would be forced "to wade through Irish blood, through the blood of the soldiers of the Irish government and through, perhaps, the blood of some of the members of the government in order to obtain Irish freedom."

These were not even partially concealed threats of what was to come if the treaty were ratified. The incitement to violence and fratricidal bloodshed filled the spring air at Killarney in County Kerry the next day when de Valera said:

> In order to achieve freedom, if our Volunteers continue until the goal is reached—if we continue on that movement which was begun when the Volunteers were started, and we suppose this treaty is ratified by your votes—then these men, in order to achieve freedom, will have, as I said yesterday, to march over the dead bodies of their brothers. They will have to wade through Irish blood.

It is curious to see de Valera, the Irish-Spanish-American, exhibiting the same blithe lack of concern for the blood of his adopted fellow countrymen as that shown by the Corsican Napoleon for adopted French blood or by the Austrian Hitler for adopted German blood. Certainly in none of these speeches does anything come through but a megalomanic desire to take the ball away at all costs from Collins and the opposition.

In spite of everything done and said by de Valera and his followers, at the general election held on June 16, 1922, their advice, suggestions, and threats were emphatically rejected. The people voted 486,419 in favor of the treaty with less than 22 percent, 133,864, voting against it.

How little concern de Valera had for the will of the people is crystal clear from two statements he made at this time. In his Killarney speech he declared that "the people have never the right to do wrong." (Doing wrong apparently meaning going counter to his wishes.) And in the Dáil he advised his associates that "reared in a labourer's cottage," not living "solely amongst the intellectuals . . . I know what I am talking about; and whenever I wanted I had only to examine my own heart and it told me straight off what the Irish people wanted."

Communing solely with his own heart, his eyes riveted on power, de Valera plunged the country headlong into civil war. The prime agent propelling the bullet that shattered the base of Michael Collins' brain in late August, 1922, two months after the general election and after Collins had become the head of state, was the hatred engendered by de Valera's violent statements the previous spring. Who pulled the trigger is still officially a mystery, but whoever it was was only an accessory after the fact.

Collins was thirty-two when he fell. He joined in death the older key leader of the Irish, the founder of the Sinn Féin Party, Arthur Griffith, at whose funeral a few weeks earlier following a brain hemorrhage he had been the chief mourner.

Up to the end Collins showed unbelievable patience toward his implacable enemies clustered under the de Valera banner. He had driven to Cork in spite of the warnings of his friends and a premonition he would be slain. The comparison to John F. Kennedy's trip to Dallas jumps to mind.

After his death, thousands filed past Collins' uniformed body lying in state at Dublin City Hall, draped with the flag of the newly born Irish Free State, a crucifix on his broad chest. The artist, John Lavery, who was granted permission to paint him as he lay there, four soldiers standing at attention by his bier through the hours of the night, wrote later: "The silence was broken at long intervals by someone entering the chapel on tiptoe, kissing the brow, and then slipping to the door where I could hear a burst of suppressed grief. One woman kissed the dead lips, making it hard for me to continue my work."

The cortege that followed Collins to the grave was the longest ever seen in Ireland. It stretched for three miles through the packed streets of Dublin, where for two agonizing years Collins had courted death at every corner. Paraphrasing Gavan Duffy's observation "No man can have two mother countries," it is hard to cherish in retrospect *both* of the Irish giants who in that tragic era finally stood face to face in mortal confrontation. It is easy to understand why there are those still alive in Ireland who hate the very name de Valera.

The Civil War continued for another nine months after the death of Collins, ending on May 24, 1923. During these months everything de Valera predicted would happen did happen, mainly because he made it inevitable that it would happen. The land ran with Irish blood. There were more murders and executions and ambushes, burnings, lootings, and armed robberies. And almost sole responsibility—no, in fact, one might just as well drop out the word "almost"—sole responsibility for what happened must rest with Eamon de Valera, for there was never an hour during those nine months when he couldn't have issued instructions which would have ended hostilities before nightfall or daybreak. He was in no way captive of an extreme wing of his faction. He ran the show and called the signals. By ceaselessly implying that there was a higher form of patriotism than cooperating with the Free State, he kept the country in a state of boiling turmoil.

In the end three factors combined to frustrate him from his purpose of immediately seizing control through violence. The Free State government, even without Collins and Griffith, with William T. Cosgrave as President and Richard Mulcahy and Kevin O'Higgins as his strong cabinet associates, rained back blow for blow upon de Valera and his supporters until they couldn't take it any longer. The Church in turn bombarded them with condemnation, and it became obvious that the vital moral support of Irish-Americans was being seriously undermined.

Even so it was with bad grace that the final submission was made. In the proclamation to his troops—whom he was still addressing as their "president"—

de Valera explained that "military victory must be allowed to rest *for the moment* with those who have destroyed the republic." (Italics the author's.) Simultaneously Frank Aiken, then de Valera's chief of staff, presently Irish Minister for External Affairs, issued an order to all ranks stating in part, "the *foreign* and *domestic* enemies of the republic have *for the moment* prevailed." (Again italics the author's.)

During those nine months Ireland lost some of her most gifted sons, on both sides of the fence, men who would have been of priceless value in the forging of a new nation. None of these men should have been sacrificed. Erskine Childers, the father of the present Minister for Power and Transportation, stood trial for illegally possessing arms, was found guilty and executed on November 24, 1922. Between then and the final submission *seventy-two others* suffered a similar fate.

At the same time the so-called Irregulars under de Valera were carrying out their announced campaign against the lives and property of members of the Dáil. Sean Hales and Padraic O'Maille, deputy chairman, were gunned down walking along the Dublin quays on December 7, 1922, Hales dying of his wounds. The Dublin house of Deputy McGarry was burned three days later, his seven-year-old son perishing from burns. Cosgrave's house was completely destroyed by fire on January 13, 1923. The following month Dr. O'Higgins, the father of Chief Justice Kevin O'Higgins, was murdered in his own home in front of his wife and daughter. It was not until four years later, on July 10, 1927, long after the Civil War —in a tragedy almost as great as the slaying of Michael

Collins—that they finally got Kevin O'Higgins himself. He was ambushed on his way home from Mass, died in his young wife's arms five hours later of eight bullet wounds.

The sensitivity of President de Valera to the historic spotlight was clearly revealed in 1967. It was announced that a panel of well-known personalities would discuss on the popular TV program "The Late Late Show" the most recent of his authorized biographies. At 6 P.M., four hours before the show was to go on, there was a terse announcement that "the discussion had been banned."

The denunciations of the hierarchy during the turbulent months of civil war—while most fortunate under the circumstances—shed considerable light on the true status of the Church in Ireland and may clarify the remark that in some ways the last half century seems like a colossal act of atonement on the part of Eamon de Valera, the relinquishing by him of temporal power as some form of penance.

On October 10, 1922, a joint pastoral was issued, which stated:

> A section of the community, refusing to acknowledge the government set up by the nation, have chosen to attack their own country as if she were a foreign power. . . . They have wrecked Ireland from end to end . . . have set out to make our motherland a heap of ruins. . . . What they call war . . . is as much murder before God as if there were no war. . . .
>
> In spite of all this sin and crime, they claim to be good Catholics and demand at the hands of the Church her most sacred privileges, like the Sacraments, reserved for her worthy members. . . .

> Vanity, perhaps self-conceit, may have blinded some who think that they, and not the nation, must dictate the national policy. . . .
>
> The guerilla warfare now being carried on by the Irregulars is without moral sanction. . . . The killing of national soldiers . . . is murder before God, the seizing of public and private property is robbery, the breaking of roads, bridges, and railways is criminal destruction, the invasion of homes and the molestation of citizens a grievous crime.
>
> All those who in contravention of this teaching participate in such crimes are guilty of grievous sins and may not be absolved in Confession nor admitted to Holy Communion if they persist in such evil actions.

The "War News" of the Irregulars in the next issue stated that de Valera had been asked to protest to the Vatican against "the unwarrantable action of the Irish hierarchy in presuming and pretending to pronounce an authoritative judgment upon the question of constitutional and political fact . . . in using the sanctions of religion to enforce their own political views . . . etc. etc."

The lenten pastorals in the next year, 1923, returned to the question of violence. That of the Archbishop of Armagh, Cardinal Logue, centered on the obscurity of de Valera's political views:

> Never before in the world's history did such a wild and destructive hurricane spring from such a thin, intangible unsubstantial vapour. The difference between some equivocal words in an oath; the difference between internal and external connection with the British Commonwealth; this is the only foundation I have ever seen alleged. Men versed in the subtleties of the schools may

> understand them; men of good, sound, practical common sense shall hardly succeed. There may be other foundations—pride, jealousy, ambition, self-interest, even mere sentimentality—but, if they exist, they are kept in the background.

With the growth of the conflict in the South, trouble erupted in the North. Unlike Michael Collins' masterful strategy against the British, it was spread all over the lot, was primarily made up of senseless terrorist attacks on the general public, further complicating the job of the new Free State, adding fuel to religious differences, and contributing its portion to the present unhappy situation.

The path taken by de Valera from armed insurrection to the attainment of power through legal means was slow and not exciting enough to trace here. His newly formed party, the Fianna Fáil, the party in control of the government today, had consistently won a number of seats in the Dáil but refused to occupy them on the grounds they wouldn't take the oath to the British government. Finally, on August 11, 1927, almost five years to the day since the death of Michael Collins, they did in fact take the oath and enter the Dáil.

It was carefully explained that de Valera had somehow always thought the oath was *really an oath* and not just a *formality* as some claimed. Having suddenly discovered himself that it was after all a formality, he decided it was time for him and his party members to sign it so they could take their places in the Dáil. They entered on the same essential terms they would have had if they had accepted Collins' original offer when the Free State was first established. During the next five years de Valera continued within the Dáil to make threats about pulling out and setting up a "republic." But as his party slowly increased its representation these threats became fainter, and when in the general election of 1932 Fianna Fáil won a clear majority and de Valera was able to form his first government, they were heard no more.

During the years since then the two major political parties have become paler and paler copies of one another, to such a degree that it takes several years of being in the country before you can tell the difference between them or even remember their names. (The other party, which stemmed out of the original Free State group, is called Fine Gael.) The very sameness of the two parties' views perhaps more than anything else illustrates how completely real power is centered somewhere else. In spite of a great deal of whooping and hollering and extensive pro and con analyses in the local press, Irish politics today are excruciatingly dull for the onlookers and one suspects for most of the participants. They are like two groups of boys in a boarding school playing at government under the benign supervision of the headmaster and faculty.

Some years ago Mr. de Valera was nudged upstairs into the Presidency, from which vantage point he pulls from time to time some of the strings which are not controlled from Maynooth, the Hierarchy's base. Two years ago the question of who would succeed Mr. Sean Lemass, who had himself succeeded Mr. de

Valera as head of the Fianna Fáil Party, came up rather suddenly with Mr. Lemass deciding to retire from politics. The logical choice was Mr. Lemass's son-in-law, Mr. Charles Haughey, who during the past five or six years has served in turn as Minister for Justice, Minister for Agriculture, and presently as Minister for Finance. As already stated, Mr. Haughey, along with the late Mr. O'Malley who apparently was felt to need more basic training, towered at the time and still towers head and shoulders above not only the members of his own party but above everybody else in Irish public life.

It so happened, however, that a few months before the question of a successor to Mr. Lemass came up Mr. Haughey had made a speech at Queen's University in Belfast, in which he stated that he felt the time had come for politicians North and South, without compromising their own long-term objectives, to try to get things off center a bit, that through closer cooperation things might be improved considerably on both sides of the Border.

With the newspapers and those in the know confidently predicting that Mr. Haughey would move unopposed into the top government spot, it suddenly became clear that he had brought down on his head the wrath of the two old-time Irregulars—President de Valera and Chief of Staff Aiken. They hastily summoned home from Chicago—where he was about to make a speech before several hundred key business executives—the Minister for Industry and Commerce, Mr. George Colley, a man of many talents and immeasurable abilities, who was hurled into the breach as an alternate candidate. A deadlock ensued—obviously as Messers de Valera and Aiken had hoped it would. Finally a compromise candidate proposed by Mr. O'Malley was chosen, Mr. Jack Lynch, then Minister for Local Affairs. Still head of the Republic, Mr. Lynch is affable, soft-spoken, thoughtful, but a totally unknown and untried political quantity.

What was most depressing about this backstairs manipulation was not that the most logical choice, Mr. Haughey, had the long, cold finger from Phoenix Park put upon him for delivering one of the few landmark speeches of this decade, but that it was painfully apparent the eight or ten "Young Turks" on the Irish scene today were woefully incapable of standing up to the longtime leaders of their party. The maneuver unfortunately also resulted in what appears to be a permanent cleavage between the two men, Haughy and Colley, who as a team could very likely resolve Ireland's unhappy predicament.

Following the example of their Honorary President, the majority of those in Irish public life appear to believe that somehow God, His appointed ministers in Ireland, and/or fate, will take care that everything in the end will turn out all right. Perhaps it's as good a way as any to run a country. But surveying what has happened during the past half century and reflecting on what might have been, the lines from Yeats's "The Rose Tree," also written in 1916, come back to mind:

*"O words are lightly spoken,"*
*Said Pearse to Connolly,*
*"Maybe a breath of politic words*

*Has withered our Rose Tree;*
*Or maybe but a wind that blows*
*Across the bitter sea."*

*"It needs to be but watered,"*
*James Connolly replied,*
*"To make the green come out again*
*And spread on every side,*
*And shake the blossom from the bud*
*To be the garden's pride."*

*"But where can we draw water,"*
*Said Pearse to Connolly,*
*"When all the wells are parched away?*
*O plain as plain can be*
*There's nothing but our own red blood*
*Can make a right Rose Tree."*

Their blood was shed, but who can truthfully claim that the Rose Tree has bloomed?

# 8

After kicking about in the accumulated rubble and debris from the last few centuries, after reflecting on the greed and brutality, the fatally short-sighted objectives, the complacent stupidity, the ignoble events and shameful episodes that made up this somber period, one might well breathe a sigh of relief and conclude that the Irish in Ireland today—God love 'em!—aren't doing a half bad job after all.

By comparison with what is happening in the outside world it is understandable too why those who have been overexposed to the hurly-burly of New York, London, Paris, Rome, and other world centers look on this slow-moving, peaceful, sea-surrounded land composed half of dreams, half of reality, as a blessed refuge from what at times takes on the proportions of a global hurricane. "And who *is* doing any better?" growls Father Garrity, glancing up from the Cork *Examiner*'s pithy rundown of the previous day's interhemispheric race riots and student rebellions.

It is only by digging back deep into the ancient

past of the Irish, by studying the evidence of the miracles they wrought in their own country before the invaders arrived on the scene, and by appreciating too what their forebears, the Celts, accomplished on the Continent, especially in France, that one awakens to a full understanding of how miserably the Irish have failed to realize their true potentials during the past half century. It is also a part of their history worth attention, because from earliest times certain racial characteristics come through which explain much in the modern Irish picture. It is impossible to understand Ireland today without taking a long look at those far-off days.

The first *accepted* ancestors of the Irish, the Celts, strode upon the world stage with a clatter and a roar that has never quite subsided. They were picked up by the spotlight of history in northern Italy about the same time they were, without benefit of any recording pens, invading Ireland—about four hundred years before Christ. They were observed pushing their way through the Alpine passes—their cattle and horses with them, their families and household possessions trundled along in large covered wagons. It was one of the greatest of all population explosions, and in a very real sense, on a planetary scale, it is still continuing.

The only historic portraits of the Celts as they were when they invaded Ireland were painted by the Romans and Greeks who brought them vividly to life from firsthand, contemporary experience. Some idea of the ferocious impact with which they must have struck Ireland is reflected by the stark terror of the Romans when the Celts descended like a tidal wave from the north, a terror that had changed slowly to cautious familiarity by the time they were more or less gracefully incorporated into the Roman Empire 350 years later.

"The whole nation is war-mad . . . high-spirited . . . quick for battle . . . otherwise simple and not uncouth." Strabo's comment covers the whole range from start to finish. They were depicted as "fair-skinned, blue-eyed, blond-haired" giants. They are "tall, muscular, and strong, our equals in valor and warlike zeal," wrote Caesar.

Centuries before the Romans and Greeks, the Celts believed in immortality, in an afterlife brimming over with pleasure and happiness. Caesar thought this was one of the chief sources of their courage, a courage that time and again on the battlefield took the form of exuberant recklessness. Valerius Maximus tells of them lending each other money that didn't need to be paid back till the next world. Posidonius describes them at a funeral, writing letters to departed comrades, then tossing the letters onto the burning pyre, the spirit of the dead man to serve as postman.

The earliest descriptions are concerned more with outer appearance than inner beliefs. There was no time for anything else. Their long, blond curls hung around the nape of the neck, and they used limewash to lighten and stiffen their hair so it would be arranged in a style similar to a horse's mane. Most of the warriors wore long, flowing moustaches which covered the mouth and reached down to the chest, as in the statue of "the Dying Gaul." (*Keltoi* in Greek and *Galli* in Latin are nearly synonymous.) The Italians were particularly horrified by the Celtic practice of suspending from their bridles the severed heads of past victims. Decapitation was practiced both on the Continent and in Ireland, with the displaying of heads a standard religious custom. Even then they were the great horsemen of Europe.

The women were also tall and muscular and often accompanied the men onto the battlefield. In the Ludovisi group of Celtic figures, the vanquished but still defiant warrior has already killed his wife and is about to commit suicide. Ammianus Marcellinus claimed that among the Celts the wife was "usually far strong' than [the husband], above all when she swells her neck, gnashes her teeth, and poising her huge arms, begins to rain down blows and kicks like shots from a catapult." He also stated that men of all ages shared the quality of bravery. "The old man marches out on a campaign with courage equal to that of the man in the prime of life."

At first it looked as though nothing would stop the Celts in Italy. The Etruscan walled towns fell one after another before them. Some historians claim it was the strong Etruscan wines that first attracted them into Italy. They were, said Appian, "intemperate by nature." They spent their leisure time roistering, feasting, drinking, and quarreling, with duels to sudden death an accepted social custom.

In 390 B.C. they inflicted a terrible defeat on the Romans at the Allia River, a tributary of the Tiber, and the legions scattered in panic across the Campania Romana. The Celts swarmed unhindered into Rome, sacked and set fire to the town, and for seven months camped in the Forum. Above them the remnants of the Roman army successfully defended the ultimate citadel, the Capitoline Hill.

One can only speculate as to what might have happened if they had taken the Capitol. The Roman Empire might well have never come into being. When one sees the ruddy Irish faces above clerical garb on the streets of Rome today, when one watches the endless streams of Irish-Americans winding through the Forum and across Michelangelo's magnificent piazza on the Capitoline Hill, it also seems as though history could have somehow been short-circuited. The Celts and the Romans, ancient adversaries, have become twin pillars of the same edifice, their descendants jointly building in the New World the most powerful stronghold of Roman Christianity. As one Irishman recently observed with a wry shake of his head, "Rome may be the Mother of the Church, but, by God, Ireland's the Mother-in-Law!"

In 279 B.C. the Celts reached their high-tide mark in Greece. Accompanied by huge, savage dogs they attacked and partially destroyed the temple at Delphi. Driven out of Greece proper they stayed on for many years in the Balkans, and in the most remarkable of all Celtic migrations pushed even farther east. Three tribes signed up as mercenaries, were given free transport to Asia Minor, where after a turbulent career as roving bandits, they settled down in northern Phrygia which was forever after called Galatia.

Some inkling as to what may have happened to earlier inhabitants in Ireland when the Celts arrived is found in Pausanias' description of the fate of the Phrygians at the hands of the same people:

> They butchered all the males, and likewise old women, and babes at their mothers' breasts; they drank

> the blood and feasted on the flesh of infants who were fat. High-spirited women, and maidens in their flower, committed suicide, while those who survived were subject to every outrage.
>
> Some of the women rushed upon the swords of the Gauls, and voluntarily courted death; to others death came from absence of food or sleep, as these merciless barbarians ravished them in turn, and wreaked their lusts upon them whether dying or dead.

In Galatia the Celts atoned for any original sins by settling down into a peaceful, productive society. Their name is associated with a number of early Christian communities who received the epistle of St. Paul. In a direct parallel to what happened in Ireland, for many centuries they retained their racial individuality, archaic customs, and their own language, in spite of being surrounded by other peoples. St. Jerome in the fourth century A.D. wrote that they spoke not only Greek but a language closely related to that of the Treveri, a Celtic tribe which dwelt along the Moselle River, a region visited by Jerome in his travels.

By 350 B.C. the Celts had conquered all of northern and north-central Italy. The entire Etruria Circumdana became Cisalpine Gaul. It was under the influence of the Etruscans that the Celts for the first, and one of the few, times in history, modified drastically their archaic, pastoral way of life, establishing major trading and dwelling centers at heavily fortified, strategic points. Turin and Milan, as well as Bologna, were founded by Celts. In Ireland the rural, dispersed, pastoral pattern of life that was typical of the first recorded Irish ancestors has been preserved almost intact up into this century. The ingrained preference of the modern Irish for cattle raising rather than tilling, for the country rather than the city, can be traced directly back to earliest times.

No major Irish city was ever established by the Irish. Dublin until 1922, when it passed from British control to the Free State, was always a "foreign" city, founded—like Wexford, Waterford, Cork, and Limerick—by the Danes, held within the Pale by the Normans and later the English. When the Irish could have had it on several occasions, they didn't want it. They let the Danes stay in possession and went on trading with them. Today with Dublin sprawling out into the country, rapidly developing characteristics "alien" to the traditional way of life that hearkens back to the good old pagan days of 400 B.C., many Irish in the West as well as in high places wish Dublin could be given back to the Danes.

The first time the Irish became urban dwellers by choice was when they migrated by the hundreds of thousands across the Atlantic to America in the nineteenth century. After years of misery and privation, culminating in the ghastly period of the Great Hunger, they had had enough of farming. Ignoring the pleas of their parish priests to return to the land, they stayed in the big cities, and it was there, forming new political, social, and economic combinations of power, that for better or worse they prospered.

This question lies at the heart of Ireland's problems today. A gigantic tug of war, mostly beneath the surface, is being waged. Today's Dublin newpapers report a speech made yesterday by a cabinet minister which couldn't be more to the point:

"We may regret the passing of the old traditions and the old customs," he said, "but merely to regret is to become a victim of what one holds on to. Farming will develop in a new and more efficient way in the West, but forestry, industry, and tourism will be needed to insure prosperity."

Each week other voices, equally if not more powerful, warn that the tried and true ways must never be abandoned. Today the same newspapers review a book just published on regional planning, the author, the Rev. Dr. Jeremiah Newman, vice-president and professor of sociology at Maynooth College.

"There is no need whatever," warns Father Newman, "for us, given the technological and sociological helps of our day, to create again the industrial monstrosities and inequities of the past, represented by uncontrolled urban-industrial growth and uninhibited commercial dominance with all its inequities and its near depravities." (Father Newman must be picturing some other country than Ireland.)

One suspects, in view of the present drift in the great European cities away from religion and toward socialism and communism, that in some minds looms the fearful image of new Turins, Milans, and Bolognas rising overnight out of the green tranquil Irish countryside.

What happened in France following Julius Caesar's defeat of the Celts is pertinent to modern Irish history. Much of the hocus-pocus about Celtic characteristics and basic traits flowed from the prolific pen of Theodor Mommsen, the nineteenth-century German historian whose favorite pastime was drawing elaborate, invidious comparisons between on the one hand the Germans and their Saxon cousins, the English, and on the other the French and *their* Celtic cousins, the Irish. Mommsen was emulated by a whole bevy of admiring English savants, inebriated on empire, plus, alas, a few Irish scholars, some of whom are still, though with less assurance, sounding the anvil chorus.

Typical of Mommsen's blind worship of the Roman ideal—which he somehow magically translated into his own private concept of the Teutonic ideal, blithely overlooking the fact that it was primarily Germanic tribes who eventually destroyed the Roman Empire—is the following passage:

> In the mighty vortex of the world's history, which inexorably crushes all nations that are not as hard and flexible as steel, such a nation [the Celts] could not permanently maintain itself. With reason, the Celts on the continent suffered the same fate at the hands of the Romans as their kinsmen in Ireland suffer down to our own day at the hands of the Saxon.

Passing over the dire consequences of Mommsen's philosophy in terms of Prussian militarism and jackbooted Nazi aspirations—not to mention the present collapsed state of the British Empire—it is worth taking a close look at exactly what "fate" the Celts "suffered at the hands of the Romans."

Not even the most rabid Celtophile could complain of how Caesar behaved after Gaul had submitted to him. He immediately embarked on a program of conciliation and friendship with his new subjects. As a result, not once during the long civil war that followed in Italy did the Celts rise in revolt. When

Caesar was securely in power at Rome, a lasting two-way partnership was formed that paid immense dividends to both parties, not the least of which was keeping the Germanic hordes out of the empire. In the following century Claudius carried out Caesar's intentions and granted the franchise to Transalpine Gaul.

Mommsen to the contrary, except for Henry VIII's enlightened approach to the Irish chiefs—and Henry was himself of Celtic (Welsh) ancestry—the long, sorry role of England in Irish affairs bears *not the slightest resemblance to the role of Rome in Gallic affairs.* The English in truth turned out to be better shopkeepers than empire builders. The suicidal colonial policy pursued by the Crown during the last half of the eighteenth century destroyed forever what could have been a solid foundation composed of the United Kingdom, Ireland, and the American colonies, a truly democratic and progressive society which in turn might have attracted other peoples throughout the world into a lasting, mutually profitable relationship. The present support in England of a partitioned Ireland is the last gasp of idiocy.

It is doubtful if any race ever accomplished as much in such a brief period of time as the Celts did in Gaul. One gets an idea of what the Irish in Ireland could do given a different set of conditions than those under which they have traditionally lived.

What happened was, in essence, a *Celtic* miracle. Worth noting is the role played by the cities, a balance which still, unlike Ireland, prevails in France. Lugdunum, the modern city of Lyons, supported a population of over 200,000 with thriving iron, ceramic, and glass industries. In pottery and weaving Gaul outstripped all other parts of the Empire. Bordeaux (Burdegala) was a bustling seaport on the Atlantic coast. Poitiers (Limonum), Clermont-Ferrand (Augustonemetum), Orléans (Cenabum) were among a score of rich inland manufacturing and trading centers, while Narbo Martius (Narbonne) on the Mediterranean was the most prosperous of all future French cities. A network of more than thirteen thousand miles of roads, built under the supervision of the Romans at first but almost entirely by Celtic hands, connected up these key urban centers.

In both town and country a solid base was created which has survived all the shocks of history, and when Rome collapsed in ruins, the ancient land of Celtica, more than any other, preserved and passed on her culture to the modern world.

One ingredient of the Celtic character which still manifests itself in Ireland emerges in ancient France. In spite of turbulence and occasional disorderliness—perhaps because of it—there is an underlying respect for authority, a willingness to accept discipline from above in place of self-discipline, which at times amounts to a fault, which takes the form of a blind unquestioning respect. Only on the rarest of occasions, under great duress, have the Irish gone against appointed authority, and then quickly, perhaps too quickly, they have returned meekly to the fold. Under Celtic law the man who broke the law was in a literal sense "excommunicated." He was cut off completely from his family and tribe, an outcast. Such a fate was considered far worse than death. Within a rigidly defined area the law inculcated a deep sense of the individual's duties and responsibilities.

Even more profound was a respect for religious authority. A great deal of nonsense has been written about the druids, but the cold facts on the Continent, and to a lesser extent in Ireland, indicate that the druidic order was the chief stabilizing force in Celtic society. They stood above the kings. No king expressed his views on any important subject until his druid had spoken, an analogy which will not be lost on those observing modern Irish politics. As a king approached old age, he was put away in a ritualistic ceremony which could only have been decreed and performed by the druids. Kingship was not inherited by the eldest son. Selection was made on the basis of merit from within the tribe, and again the decision must have rested to a large extent with the priestly class.

The druids were not only responsible for religious training but were in charge of *all* education, another situation with a familiar ring. They were probably the only literate members of the community. Belief in an afterlife must have stemmed from them. They were the judges, kept the historic records, studied the stars, and devised the calendars. When St. Columba in A.D. 575, during the great convention at Bruim Cead in Ireland, successfully urged that the druidic order of bards, the Filid, be admitted into the framework of Christianity, he not only helped strengthen the position of the Church, he insured the preservation of the oral traditions, the legends, and the poems for another thousand years.

The druids were, significantly, not an hereditary class. With the nobles, from whom the kings were selected, and the freeman commoners, mostly farmers and some craftsmen, they formed a threefold society—a "social and religious entity" in which all persons were "free and sacred." Even the land was not owned by an individual but by the kin from whom it could never be parted. In many respects the archaic Celtic society was communal in nature, and this is still apparent in the relatively "classless" aspect of modern Irish society.

In France the druidic order was quietly suppressed during the first century after Caesar. Roman gods and goddesses became interfused with pagan. Unlike Ireland where the transition was direct, there was a five-hundred-year interval between Druidism and Christianity. Roman law also replaced Celtic law in France within the first hundred years, and as the power of the kings, the support of their druids gone, slowly waned, the rise of the nobles presaged the feudal age. With the blending of the Celtic society into other ways of life on the Continent, it was only in Ireland that their traditional way of life prevailed.

Each year facts pile up on top of facts which indicate that the two thousand years *prior* to the arrival of the Celts in Ireland may well be the most fascinating period in Irish history, may well answer the riddle of why the Irish are such a complex race. In November, 1967, the *Sunday Times* magazine (London) referred to "historical remains unique in scope and expression" which point toward the existence in Ireland of "highly sophisticated societies at a time when across the Irish Sea men were grubbing about in the dirt or fighting for a living with a horizon no more distant than the next hill."

During those far-off centuries a fairly large population enjoyed prosperity, peace, and undisputed control of Ireland. It stands to reason that certain strong racial characteristics were formed in the Irish which can't be explained in terms of what is known of the Celts on the Continent. It is becoming more and more apparent that the Irish represent a split racial personality—Celt and pre-Celt.

Edmund Curtis, the distinguished Trinity College, Dublin, historian, estimated that *as late as* A.D. *800*, after having been in Ireland for twelve hundred years, the Celts were still a *minority* race, their culture forcibly imposed on top of an earlier, and in many respects a superior civilization. Yet so enamored are the Irish with being "Celtic," so apparently loath are they to delve into their prehistoric genealogy for fear of what they'll find, that these pre-Celts remain the *forgotten Irish*.

Where the mysterious pre-Celtic basic ingredient in the Irish race came from is a subject of hot contention today, with more and more evidence pointing toward the Mediterranean, an origin which is anathema to the old-line Celtophiles. These early Irish people were short, long headed, dark complexioned, much like the type of person found in Spain today, the direct antithesis of the "blond, fair-haired" Celts on the Continent. C. H. V. Sutherland, in his fascinating book *Gold*, labels one chapter "From Ur to Ireland," then develops the theory that the search for gold, after the Egyptians cornered the crude-ore supply in their part of the world, sent others from the neighboring areas, including Chaldea, first to Crete, then westward to the Spanish (Iberia) peninsula, hence to Ireland (Hibernia) where the Wicklow supplies were discovered.

Irish mythology tends to support a dual, totally dissimilar ancestry. The first cycle contains the great seafaring tales, epic in spirit, overflowing with the same release from the bondage of earth found in *The Odyssey*. They tell, as do the Greek legends, of enchantments and transformations, of distant islands of immortality across the sea. They center around the gigantic figure of Manannán mac Lir, God of the Sea, the Outer King of Ireland, the "best pilot in the West of Europe," the "reknowned trader." *Inis Manan*, the Isle of Man, was named after him. More than any other mythological figure he assumed natonal stature throughout Ireland and Great Britain.

There is one highly intriguing facet to a Mediterranean origin that cannot be ignored, although it gets short shrift in academic Dublin. It is generally agreed that both English and insular Celtic—Irish, Welsh, and Scotch—contain a sizable *common* substratum which predates the two languages.

A small group of embattled but extremely well-positioned scholars, spearheaded by Dr. Professor Julius Pokorny, considered by many the greatest living Celtic authority, at eighty still active with the Institute of Comparative Etymology in Zurich, and Professor H. H. Wagner, head of the Department of Celtic Studies at Queen's University, Belfast, maintain that this common substratum is not only of Mediterranean origin, but, opening up a door leading to even more distasteful vistas as far as the traditionalists are concerned, they believe it is closely related to Berber, Egyptian, and Hebrew.

To put it bluntly, they claim that the original blood stock in England, Ireland, Scotland, and Wales is Jewish.

This avenue was first explored by a Welsh professor named Maurice-Jones, who at the turn of the century published a lengthy tract setting forth similarities in syntax between Welsh and certain Berber dialects. According to Dr. Wagner, Maurice-Jones' theory was "not welcomed with open arms." It is almost impossible to locate a copy of Maurice-Jones' article today in either England or Ireland. Celtophiles and Anglophiles alike have been content to let things rest as they are. This specter of an unwished-for heritage lurking in the wings may account in part for the anti-Mediterranean attitude prevalent in polite classical circles. But one cannot shrug off the research of Maurice-Jones, Pokorny, Wagner, and others.

The blending of the Celts with this earlier, apparently more highly developed civilization in Ireland resulted in a golden age which surpassed anything contemporary to it in Western Europe. While the fact isn't bruited about in Ireland today, this golden age, lasting from about the fifth century A.D. to the ninth century A.D., took place outside the orbit of the Church of Rome. Not only outside, but in competition with, often in direct opposition to Rome.

If the organizing abilities of the Irish had equaled their faith, learning, and missionary zeal, they might have anticipated by many hundreds of years Bernard Shaw, who predicted that, once free, the twentieth-century Irish would establish the spiritual center of the West in Dublin. Depending on the future course of Continental events, it could still happen. Remoteness might again become an asset.

Perhaps it is an error to limit the golden age of Ireland to those four historic centuries. It must have started to take shape, to form its vital elements, several centuries before Christ. The entire period from 400 B.C., to A.D. 795, when the first Viking raid struck Lambay Island just north of Dublin like sudden lightning out of the blue sea, can best be regarded as one uninterrupted national flow of life. During those twelve centuries, with an impetus that carried over during another century of invasions, Irish traditions and beliefs, spirit, culture, language, learning, and creative imagination came into being under paganism, then flowered in the warm glow of early Christianity.

It was an age of such a nature that if a comparable one were created in Ireland today, few could ask for more. A deep, partly unconscious yearning for such an age is one reason so many of the modern Irish shy away from material progress, why so many speeches and sermons are hurled at the gods of Mammon. It is the theme of Denis Johnson's superb play of the 1920's, *Moon in the Yellow River*, which found such an immense response among nuclear-age Americans in New York a few seasons ago.

The far-off past, except for certain somewhat shocking aspects, has not been forgotten, although the actual facts have become muddied. A considerable portion of the population fear that in the struggle for worldly benefits the dream of an Irish rebirth of spiritual, intellectual, and artistic well-being will vanish. They believe—and they believe that what has happened in the rest of the world proves beyond any argument—that you simply can't have both types of civilizations. Ask the average native, for example, if he'd like to live in a setup roughly comparable to the one so many millions of migratory Irish have helped build in America. All you have to do is read a few Irish books and articles on the subject, see a few Irish plays, which portray their American "cousins"—the cigar-smoking, sport-shirted, Cadillac-driving tycoons with their inevitable martini-drinking, neurotic, heaven-only-knows-perhaps-secretly-adulterous-in-thought-if-not-in-deed wives—to get a speedy answer to *that* question. Personally I am convinced that, *given the prevailing set of conditions,* the Irish have about as much chance of creating another golden age as they have of being the first nation to reach the moon. But at least they know what they *don't* want.

A glance at the population-per-square-mile figures for Europe gives some idea of how drastically the future of Ireland can still be fashioned by the Irish. Ireland is approximately one eighth that of England's, Holland's, and Belgium's. To bring it up even with the average for Europe would mean tripling it. A splendid mark to shoot at in the next fifty years would be to equal France and Denmark, which would mean doubling the population. Recently an American magazine stated flatly that the Irish had given up sex, that they weren't having children anymore. Using the Roman Catholic Church as an operating instrument, they had "emasculated" themselves. While this makes sensational reading, such are not the facts. In 1965, when the last census was taken, the Irish birth rate per thousand stood at 22.1, compared to 18.1 for England and Wales which is published as a joint figure. Each year for the past fifty years the Irish have produced about 64,000 new Irish. At that rate the population would just about double in the next fifty years, if some way could be found to keep the Irish in Ireland, which in itself implies sweeping social and economic changes. Each year the same approximate number of Irish leave as arrive. About half, 33,000, die. The rest migrate.

Turning from such mundane but highly pertinent matters back to Ireland's past, the more one explores into Irish mythology the more obvious it becomes that a split racial personality is involved. In the second, so-called Heroic Cycle, we leave behind peace and plenty, the traditions of a seafaring people, the wizards, men of intelligence, the traders and craftsmen who dominate the first cycle, and are back with the same Celtic warriors who stood forth from their chariots at Telamon and other Continental battlefields and hurled fierce challenges at the Romans.

As one would expect in the legends of a conquering people holding a larger subject population in check, the emphasis is constantly on unswerving devotion to duty, the protagonists guided by a strict code of personal honor. Time and again the heroes are faced with two choices, either of which can only lead to disaster. Fergus, the deposed king of Ulster, must either be disloyal to the troops serving under him or fight both his stepson Conchobar and his adored foster son CúChulainn. In turn, CúChulainn is forced through duty to slay his once closest friend, FerDaid, and later his own son Conlaí.

It is understandable why most scholars believe this group of legends was never popular with the common people. They were apparently composed with the Celtic nobles as patrons. The brutally uncompromising, almost heartless philosophy, may strike you as very un-Irish, yet these tales are tragic counterparts to the tumultuous events of the first half of this century in Ireland, events which illustrate that nothing should come as a surprise among the Irish.

There has been no morning since I have been here

that I would have been startled to awake and find that some sense of duty, on the part of an individual or a group, smoldering unsuspected under the surface, had suddenly burst into flaming headlines. The Irish people, the vast majority of them, could not have been more stunned, or for that matter outspokenly indignant, when savage rebellion focused world attention on Dublin that lovely, calm Holy Easter weekend in 1916.

During the Troubles and the Civil War, the Irish leaders found themselves again and again in situations where they followed duty to no matter what tragic end it led, acting directly counter to normal Irish family and religious training. When Dan Breen, "the man who started the war," as Michael Collins called him, blew up the first dynamite-laden munitions cart, filling the mild Tipperary air with pieces of the accompanying Royal Irish Constable—when Collins ordered every known British secret agent in Dublin, with or without wife or mistress, murdered in bed on Bloody Sunday morning, thus effectively "gouging out the eyes of the English in Ireland"—when hostages and suspected traitors were shot dead on tramcars, in crowded streets, and at lonely houses, these men were calling on an inner strength which flowed directly from the Heroic legends, a hidden strength which no one—the English, wives and sweethearts, fellow countrymen, bishops and earls, not even the men themselves—had suspected was there.

The bulk of the literature of the Troubles is concerned with this theme of grim duty—Liam O'Flaherty's *The Informer*, much of Sean O'Casey's finest material including *Shadow of a Gunman*, as well as such dramas by others as *The Iron Harp, Odd Man Out,* and *Shake Hands with the Devil,* where the young Irish-American sympathizer finds himself in just such a torturous predicament: "Are his convictions so strong he will go against his normal principles and kill a man?" The bullet-riddled end of Cathal Brugha outside the blazing wreck of the Hamman Hotel in Dublin was compared by Frank O'Connor to the death of CúChulainn, the mightiest of Irish champions, "tying himself to a pillarstone by his belt and facing his enemies until the battle glory faded from his head and the bird of evil omen perched upon the bowed shoulder."

The tragedy of modern Ireland is brought into sharp relief by the fact that the founding members of the Irish Republican Brotherhood in the nineteenth century chose their name, the Fenians, from the *third,* the so-called Fenian Cycle of mythology, and that the inexorable force of destiny ruled that those who successfully fulfilled their mission in this century had to revert to the philosophy of the *second* cycle in order to carry out their objectives in the face of harsh reality. Thus reversing the evolutionary process which led to Ireland's golden age. For in the earlier progression from the Heroic tales to the Fenian tales, we watch the *descendants* of the people in the first cycle emerge back into the light of day, and the soul of Ireland miraculously comes into being. We witness the conquered winning out over their conquerors, the Celts, or at least establishing with them a satisfactory *modus operandi.* The distinctive quality of these Fenian myths, or half-myths, has been described as "human warmth of feeling," compared to "intelligence and knowledge" in the first group, "willpower, honor, and duty" in the second.

All the elements found in the age of chivalry, in the ballads of the troubadours, in the best of medieval literature—romantic love, the joys of hunting and of fairs, the passion for nature and the Irish countryside—unfold in the Fenian Cycle like petals on a newly created flower. Their influence is still profoundly felt in Ireland today by both the people and the poets. The legends of King Arthur and the Knights of the Round Table, as well as the stories of Robin Hood and his men of the green forests, have been traced back to this brimming fountainhead. It was the same rich source which played a key role in sparking off the great Celtic revival of the late nineteenth century, which inspired some of the finest efforts of such poets and playwrights as William Butler Yeats, James Stephens, Lady Gregory, Douglas Hyde, Austin Clarke, Lord Dunsany, and many others.

Heroes are again the principal characters in the Fenian tales but of a completely different type from the second cycle. They were "chosen bodies of fine young men," motivated by "heroism, gentleness, and justice." They used force only to oppose force and to keep the peace. They fought in groups rather than as individual champions, never from chariots like the Celts, usually on foot but sometimes mounted.

The Fenians lived outside the settled regions, inhabiting "the rivers, the wastes, the wilds, and the woods, the precipices and estuaries." Their traditions were linked back to bygone heroes and far-off places across the sea. They overflowed with the spirit of camaraderie and knew the "intense pleasure shared with one's own special group . . . in marked contrast to the harsh individuality which characterizes so many of the Ulster (heroic cycle) stories." The delights of these early Irishmen are described in a famous passage by Oisin or Ossian, the son of Finn Mac Cool, the warrior leader of the bands:

> The music that Finn loved was that which filled the heart with joy and gave light to the countenance, the song of the black bird of Letter Lee, and the melody of the Dord Fian, the sound of the wind in Droum-Derg, the thunders of Assaroe, the cry of the hounds let loose through Glen Ra, with their faces outward from the Suir, the Tonn Rury lashing the shore, the wash of water against the side of ships, the cry of Bran at Knock-an-awr, the murmur of streams at Slieve-Mish and oh, the black bird of Derry-Cairn. I never heard, by my soul, sound sweeter than that. Were I only beneath his nest!

The sounds of the chase echo down the centuries unchanged from what they are today. One summer afternoon Finn stretches out on the hill of Knockainy near the little modern village of Hospital in County Limerick while his companions hunt on the plain below:

> And it was sweet music to Finn's ear the cry of the long-snouted dogs as they routed the deer from their covers and the badgers from their dens; the pleasant shouts of the youths, the whistling and signalling of the huntsmen, and the encouraging cheers of the he-

roes, as they spread themselves through the glens and woods, and over the broad, green plain of Cliach.

Elsewhere one hears the "musical concert of three packs of hounds hunting round the head of Sliabh Lugda . . . the melodious chase by beagles after the swift and gentle hares . . . the shout of the gillies, and the fastest of the boys, and the readiest of the warriors, and the men who were the straightest spear shots, and the strong attendants who bore the heavy burdens."

Besides Finn Mac Cool and his son Oisin, the Fenians included "the brave and gentle Oscar," son of Oisin; Goll McMorna, the "mighty leader of the Connacht Fena"; the "swift-footed" Cailte MacRonan, and Dermot O'Dyna, "unconquerably brave, of untarnished honor, generous and self-denying," termed by the late P. W. Joyce of Trinity College, Dublin—"the finest character in all Irish literature, perhaps the finest in any literature."

Of the Fenian legends Dr. Whitley Stokes, whose monumental work included over forty published books and treatises on the Irish, wrote: "The tales are generally told with sobriety and directness . . . they evince genuine feeling for natural beauty, a passion for music, a moral purity, a noble love for manliness and honor . . . [they are] admirable for their unstudied pathos." Dr. Kuno Meyer spoke of their "purity, loftiness, and tenderness."

This is all the more remarkable because these legends are pre-Christian in origin. They not only are full of pagan allusions and philosophical concepts, but it is possible to date them to at least the third century A.D., two hundred years before St. Patrick undertook his mission in Ireland. Finn Mac Cool and his men were in the service of Cormac Mac Art, the first great historic Irishman, High King from A.D. 218 to A.D. 260. The earliest reliable date for St. Patrick's mission is A.D. 432.

It is not overstating the case to say that only Cormac Mac Art and Brian Boru in the tenth century came even close to forming an Irish nation before the Free State came into being in 1922. Two men in two thousand years! Like Brian Boru, Cormac put a temporary end to the regional bickerings and petty wars between local kings which plagued Ireland long after the Vikings, Normans, and English were in the land, a sectionalism which still characterizes Irish politics.

Nor is it overstating the case to say that the soul of ancient Ireland was breathed into an extremely lusty, vigorous, earthy body. To dispel the misty, widely held concept of the entire early Irish population, men and women, strolling about in neoclassical, diaphanous white gowns, illuminated manuscripts tucked under their arms, exchanging passages of mellifluous verse, strumming harps and chanting hymns, it is necessary to touch on a few violently contradictory highlights.

If those who today yearn for a return to Ireland's golden age were magically granted their wish, but had to take the bad with the good, to accept the entire package, many would unquestionably, on reflection, flatly turn down the offer.

Judged by modern Irish standards, morals were atrocious. Divorce was common practice. Elopements involving married women, the open living together of lovers with frequent switches of partners, an appalling number of illegitimate children—these were all conspicuous elements in the early Irish social pattern. The keeping of concubines—young girls who served as mistresses, prostitutes, and second wives—was especially prevalent among the upper classes and apparently not looked upon with disfavor by the general public. One of the few abuses singled out by St. Patrick in his *Confessio* was "the sad lot of slave girls" who provided a ready source of supply for a waiting market.

It may seem strange that such outrageous customs were widespread in a country where purity of thought, romantic love, and loftiness of purpose had blossomed into exquisite poetry and folklore, a country where certain classes of women enjoyed unique privileges and were granted extraordinary marks of respect. The evidence, however, from the legends, from the great mass of written law surviving from the period, and from the subjects listed on the agendas of early Church assemblies, leaves no possible room for doubt in these matters.

Even worse, such conditions not only flourished during pagan times and were the rule of the land in the fifth century A.D. when St. Patrick undertook his mission, but during the next seven hundred years of Christianity, things did not improve to any noticeable degree. As in many youthful, expanding civilizations, immorality and virtue rubbed shoulders side by side. The identification of sex as sin, within the Christian community, was a lengthy, slow process.

The extent to which Puritanism conquered Ireland—far more than what happened in France, Italy, and even Spain, the three principal Continental countries which remained Roman Catholic throughout the Reformation—can be partially attributed to the freewheeling licentiousness which prevailed in earlier times and the lengths to which the Church went to curb these hearty appetites. Ireland was the only Roman Catholic country which in the end outpuritaned the Puritans. The pent-up, "seething beneath the surface" characteristics of more than one present-day Irishman, or Irishwoman, which are inclined to flare up under the stimulation of strong alcoholic beverages or on removal from strict clerical discipline, can be traced back in part to the original uninhibited habits of the race. The Irish are not docile or god-fearing by nature. It has taken over a thousand years to make them what they are. At times even those in charge of the long-term program must be secretly astonished at how successful celibate mind has been over turbulent matter.

Of their own people the Irish sold only illegitimate children into slavery, which compared favorably with their British neighbors. Large numbers of legitimate English children and unwanted relations were disposed of at auction, particularly at the great Bristol slave mart. A high percentage were bought and taken home by the Irish. All or most of the slaves imported into Ireland came from Britain. St. Patrick first arrived in Ireland as a fourteen-year-old slave taken in a coastal raid most likely in Scotland or Wales. St. Brigid, his celebrated native Irish disciple, was illegitimate, the daughter of a slave and a chieftain named Dubthach. While many Celtic nobles embraced Christianity, bringing their followers into the fold with them, there must have been, as in pagan Rome, a ready welcome at the lower levels of society for a new religion offering hope and eternal resurrection. Yet this acceptance at both the top and the bottom made little change in daily habits or in the practice of slavery. At the Synod of Armagh in 1171, a year after the arrival of the Normans, the clergy concluded that the invasion was a curse brought down from Heaven as a punishment for "the inhuman traffic in slaves." It was decreed that all *English* slaves should be set free and allowed to return to their own country, but no mention was made of native-born slaves. Another major item on the same agenda was the "distressing state of marital relations." The following year, at the Council of Cashel, it was decreed that "all the faithful throughout Ireland shall eschew concubinage with their cousins and kinfolk, and contract and adhere to lawful marriages."

In sharp contrast to the somewhat dubious status of women from the lower classes, those from the middle and upper classes were entitled to what can fairly be described as equal rights. In many ways they fared considerably better than their counterparts in other European countries. When a woman entered marriage, her own property—gold and jewelry, land, herds of cattle—continued to be hers. Separate accounts were kept, and when and if the marriage was dissolved, she took with her what was rightfully hers. This was subject to court procedure in which the wife's testimony was held to be on a par with her husband's. In matters of property it was an extremely meticulous society.

There were seven valid grounds for granting a wife a divorce. Aside from the usual reasons of abandonment and infidelity she could win her freedom if she could prove that "the husband had inflicted upon her through beating a visible bruise or blemish . . . if he had made her the subject of ridicule in public . . . and if he had denied her full rights in domestic and social matters." Amplifying the last point, the law decreed, "Every noble woman is entitled to the exercise of her own free will."

A number of careers were open to women at all levels. Mention is made of celebrated women lawyers and physicians as well as scholars. The death of Uallach, chief poetess of Ireland in A.D. 983 is noted in one manuscript. Young girls, chiefly from the noble class, attended the monastic schools.

In a direct carry-over from Caesar's time the Irish women still accompanied their men into battle. It was not until A.D. 697, 250 years after St. Patrick, that a meeting of laymen and clergy at Tara officially exempted women from military services. More than one long-limbed Amazon must have hung up her scarred battle shield and stored away her sword and spears with a sigh of regret. The clergy too marched off to war with the armed forces but they were let off a century after the women, in A.D. 803.

There were still many opportunities for robust contact between the sexes. As is true today, the stimulating, blood-warming atmosphere of the hunting field seems to have sparked off a number of assignations and elopements. As late as the sixteenth century the fabulous Grace O'Malley, "Queen of Galway," who became a warm friend of Elizabeth I, disdained stirrups and saddle, riding bareback and astride in the approved Irish fashion. Women were regularly invited along on the perpetual cattle raids which one writer has described as only slightly bloodier than present-day fox-hunting.

At Tara the women had their own banquet hall, but elsewhere they feasted and drank with the men. The precedence of the wives was a source of constant jealousy and bickering. In some cases the women sat at a separate table wearing masks and veils, but in "The Vision of Cahirmore" the two sexes got so drunk together they all fell into a deep sleep during which someone slipped in and stole the golden diadem off the queen's head. In another tale Feldelma, the young comely wife of a warrior, has to leave the hall "with her fifty handmaidens," suffering from "heaviness of drink." When St. Patrick made his way for the first time up the hill to Tara, which happened to be on Easter Sunday morning, it is said he found a riotous, all-night party still in full swing.

Far and away the most charming and informative vignettes of Irish life during those relatively carefree centuries are found in the descriptions of the great annual fairs. Here the general public had their only chance to meet face to face. The fairs constituted the one communal aspect in an otherwise dispersed existence. Most of these huge gatherings had originated in prehistoric times as funeral games but, like race meetings and country fairs today, they became the gayest and most colorful of all Irish spectacles.

Every class of person in Ireland, high or low, rich or poor, turned up at the fairs. It was a religious obligation, the forerunner of today's pilgrimages to holy places. Those held at Tlachtga and Ushnagh remained primarily spiritual in nature, but at the others there were "games and races, pleasure and amusement, eating and feasting." Cormac's Glossary from the ninth century lists under *Aenach* (Fair), "Food and precious raiment, downs and quilts, ale and flesh-meat, chessmen and chess boards, horses and chariots, greyhounds and playthings besides."

From the opening of a fair until the close there were rigidly enforced rules of conduct. Fines were imposed for "brawling, quarreling, or noisy drunkenness." Serious infringements were punishable by death. The universal fair truce, identical to the armistice at the Olympian and Isthmian games, was sacred in origin. So rarely were major crimes committed that they were recorded in the manuscripts, as when "Fogartach [Fogarty] O'Carney disturbed the fair of Taillten, for he murdered Maekruba, son of Dubhsleibhe."

All feuds and grudges were for the moment to be put aside. Any actions likely to create new frictions, "such as elopements, repudiations of wives by husbands, or vice versa," had to be postponed to another day. Fresh seeds might be sown but not reaped. No legal action could be taken against debtors. No matter how heavily involved a man might be, he could enjoy himself as much as the wealthiest cattle owner or the most powerful chieftain, free from any danger of arrest or bodily injury.

With chariots, mounted horsemen, and persons on

foot congregating by the thousands, there were as many chances for collisions as today. "Provision was made that in case a chariot should be broken, or anyone was injured by furious driving, or should any other accident occur, the person responsible should be made liable, but should at the same time be protected from vexatious prosecutions."

Taillten, held annually on the last day of July and the first two days of August was the largest and most popular of the fairs, with people streaming in from all over Ireland and as far away as Scotland. At the final official gathering in 1169, presided over by Rory O'Connor, the last *native* High King of Ireland, the horses and chariots were backed up in an unbroken line to Kells, six miles away, which sounds like Fairyhouse on the day of the Irish Grand National.

Taillten was famous for its games and athletic competitions, the closest thing to National Olympics, with teams and champions defending their laurels against younger challengers. Weddings were another feature. Since most marriages were arranged, the young men and girls were kept apart in separate places while the parents did their bargaining on Tulach-na-Coibche, "the hill of the buying," where the price for the bride was paid. The ceremonies were performed in a nearby glen called the Marriage Hollow. Both hollow and hill can be seen to this day. If a couple who married failed to make a success of the venture, they could return to the hollow, stand back to back, one facing north, the other south, then walk off, free of all bonds, in opposite directions.

A poem composed by a bard named Fulartach about A.D. 1000 and included in the Book of Leinster gives, along with several other shorter poems, an especially vivid picture of contemporary Irish life in its description of the triennial Carman Fair. This was held primarily for the people of Leinster and lasted six days. Forty-seven local chiefs with their followers regularly attended. Each of the chiefs had his allotted place at the meetings held daily in the council house, and he clung to his rights as jealously as any dowager countess at court. The King of Leinster presided in the center, the King of Ossory on his right, the King of Offaly on his left, and so on down the line. The council also included the brehons, or lawmakers, and in earlier times the druids. Questions involving fiscal, legal, and other matters affecting the next three years were raised and settled.

The women had their own daily assemblies where subjects of special feminine interest were discussed. Each sex was barred from the other's meetings. In gatherings open to both sexes the women sat with their husbands, which simplified the problem of precedence. There was a full schedule for women aside from the conferences. Sports called "the games of the women of Leinster"—with "the people of Leix" assigned the ticklish responsibility of refereeing the matches—were held late each afternoon. The referees also took charge of the jewelry which "the Leinster women wore in abundance and which they had to lay aside during the course of the games." There were other events for different tribes and classes. The people of Ossory had a day reserved for what was called the "steed contest of the Ossorians," in which chariots as well as mounted horsemen competed. On another day only the Roydamas, or "crown princes" were allowed to enter the games.

The fairs were a pageant of brilliant colors and the latest fashions, for the women worked all year preparing new wardrobes:

> The people were dressed in their best, and in great variety . . . from head to foot every individual wore articles of varied hues. Here you see a tall gentleman walking along with a scarlet cloak flowing loosely over a short jacket of purple, with perhaps blue trousers and yellow headgear, while the next showed a colour arrangement wholly different; and the women vied with the men in variety of hues. Nay, single garments were often parti-coloured; and it was quite common to see the long outside mantle, whether worn by men or women, striped with purple, yellow, green, or other dyes.

The bards came to the fairs from all corners of the land. There were recitations and contests featuring new stories and poems, as well as the traditional favorites, some dating back to the early funeral games. "A never-wearying entertainment: stories of destruction, cattle-preys, courtships, rhapsodies, battle-odes, royal precepts, and the truthful instruction of Fithil the Sage: poets and learned men with their tablets and books of trees: deep poetry, and Dinsenchus or History of Places: the wise precepts of Carbery and Cormac mac Airt."

The long summer hours were flooded with music—harps, bagpipes, trumpets, wide-mouthed horns and fiddles. Mention is made of "bone-men" (castenet players), "tube-players" and "chain-men" who apparently shook music out of linked metal rings from which bells dangled. Historians have been puzzled by the total absence of any mention of dancing.

In one section people milled closely around "showmen, jugglers, and clowns with grotesque masks or painted faces . . . all bellowing out their rude jests to the laughing crowds . . ." for there were "professors of every art, both the noble arts and the base arts." Among the occupations listed in the ancient lawbooks is "equestrians"—those who stand on the backs of horses at the fairs."

Another important area was set aside as a huge bazaar for buying and selling. There were three types of markets—"a market of food and clothes: a market of livestock and horses; an enclosure for foreign merchants with gold and silver and fine raiments to sell." One hill was known as the slope of the embroidering women, where work was done in front of the people and offered for sale as it was finished. The great bulk of articles bought and sold during an entire year changed hands at the fairs. Elsewhere there was a major catering operation in progress with food cooked and served to the vast crowds.

On the final day of the fair, prizes, usually gold rings, were awarded to the winners of the contests, the presentations made by well-known leaders of the people. "When the evening of the last day had come, and all was ended, the men of the entire assembly stood up and made a great clash with their spears, each man striking the handle of the next man's spear with the handle of his own: which was the signal for the crowd to disperse." With the introduction of

Christianity in the fifth century, each day began with a religious ceremony, and the day after the fair there was usually a Mass, but otherwise there was little change from prehistoric times.

Today the elements of the great fairs are still part of the Irish scene but usually broken down into separate occasions—into mammoth annual pilgrimages, into greyhound and horse racing, football and hurling matches, weekly and monthly livestock markets, special events such as the Waterford Music Festival and the Dublin Theater Festival. And yet at scores of small annual fairs and at a number of two-day and three-day country race meetings—at Tralee, Listowel, Galway, Mallow, and Killarney—one can still recapture intact the exuberant spirit, the many-faceted nature of Taillten and Carman. A point-to-point meeting or even the smallest gymkhana, virtually unpublicized, will pull together out of thin air a sizable crowd as well as a band of tinkers and peddlers who swiftly set up brightly colored booths offering wares for sale and a choice of rather questionable games of chance. The eager attendance at these local affairs testifies to the isolation in which the Irish continue to live during most of the year.

Turning over again the kaleidoscope of Ireland as it was before the invasions began, one can observe a phenomenon peculiar to any developing society, any awakening people—an explosion taking place simultaneously in a number of directions. It cannot be channeled. One of necessity must take the bad with the good. Man's glorious moments have not been experienced in a straitjacket. Only when inspiration has flagged and soaring free thought has dropped back to earth comes a weighing up, a sorting out of values, a time to conserve. During golden ages, paradox and seeming contradiction call the tune while cautious, orderly minds despair.

This was true during the classical age of Greece, in the pulsating turmoil of ancient Rome's greatness, in the liberal, deeply stirred but prematurely stifled twelfth century, during the Renaissance with Cellinis briefly glimpsed in street brawlings and tavern stabbings, in the Elizabethan Age and the last half of the eighteenth century in England—perhaps most pertinent of all it was true during the first fifty years after Spain's liberation from the Moors, when visionary saints, both men and women, and divinely inspired writers and artists emerged from the same womb as ruthless empire builders.

Given the present intellectual and cultural climate in Ireland, the dread of change, the web softly spun around each individual, the fear of God and hell—rather than the love of God and heaven and this earth—ingrained from childhood in every Irish person—given these conditions which are the exact opposite to those which prevailed in ancient Ireland, those who today wait for another golden age wait in vain. If it were going to happen, it would have started to happen during the past half century. That it hasn't rests on the heads of those who have created the climate, who have drawn up and enforced the rules. Not to mention those who have laid supine at their feet.

Against the background of an already awakened poetic spirit, rampant earthiness, and a fierce partisan sense of independence, the advent of Christianity in

Ireland triggered off in other directions what was in the truest sense of the word a revolution. In their unquenchable thirst for knowledge, in their refusing to be corseted into narrow orthodoxy, in their passionate enthusiasm for their new faith and their desire to tell everyone else about it, in their discovery of divinely inspired beauty in the world around them and their ability to fashion out of this beauty fresh forms of artistic expression, certain of the early Irish lifted their age up in their own hands, with their own minds and spirits and fashioned it into one of the most splendid achievements ever created on this earth. They didn't do so by preserving the status quo. In spite of all the fulsome praise and endless prattling about "the good old days," what these early Irishmen actually accomplished—and *how* and *why*—has long since been forgotten or ignored.

A whole world lies between the approaches to Christianity of St. Patrick and Johannes Erigena, far and away the most intelligent Irishman of all times. The former, in his unshakable faith and gifted with what must have been unbelievable powers of persuasion, was directly or indirectly responsible for more converts to Christ than any other person except St. Paul. Erigena, a ninth-century layman, has been universally acclaimed as the most original thinker born between classical times and the Renaissance, "a man whose existence casts doubt upon the advisability of retaining the phrase 'Dark Ages' even for the ninth century." Yet Patrick and Johannes are both integral parts of the same miracle, the miracle that took place in Ireland during the first five centuries of Christianity.

St. Patrick's conversion of the Irish set off a chain reaction that swept into first western then eastern Scotland, southward into Northumbria (for more than a century the Northumbrian kings spoke Irish), on to the Thames, through East Anglia and Mercia as far west as Glastonbury. It crossed open ocean to the Orkneys, the Hebrides, the Shetlands. When the Vikings discovered Iceland in A.D. 870, they also discovered Christians who had "departed and left behind them Irish books, bells, and other things, from whence it may be inferred that these Christians were Irish" (Zeuss, *Grammatica Celtica*).

Another irresistible wave rolled across the Continent, into Burgundy, Switzerland, Austria, Bavaria, Frisia, Saxony, and over the Alps into Lombardy. Far more Europeans were brought into the Christian fold by the Irish than by the Romans. Later the Italians came north and shepherded these converts of St. Patrick under the banner of St. Peter, in the end capturing the recalcitrant Irish themselves.

Thomas Dempster, the seventeenth-century Scottish historian who helped lead the Etruscans into the academic limelight, tried to do a comparable job for the followers of St. Patrick on the false assumption they were fellow Scots. As soon as it was irrefutably proved that the vast majority were—God help us!—native Irishmen, the scholars of the eighteenth century, at least those writing in English, unceremoniously dumped them back into the pool of oblivion. From which no one—including the Irish, except for paying them meaningless lip service—have bothered to rescue them. The very fact that they *were* in competition with Rome would seem to account for the fact that outside of their names nine out of ten present-day educated Irish men and women know nothing of their accomplishments.

Ignorance in Great Britain on the subject is, if possible, even more profound. St. Andrew, patron saint of Scotland, and St. George, patron saint of England, had no more to do with those two countries than St. Paul had to do with prehistoric days in Minnesota. St. Andrew was born in the tiny fishing village of Capernaum on the Sea of Galilee, and is believed to have been crucified at Patras in western Greece. He never came within a thousand miles of the cathedral, university, and golf club which bear his name. Some claim there was a St. George who was put to death at Lydda in Palestine but the consensus is that he never existed. Dr. Peter Heylyn, the seventeenth-century Oxford historian who spent years of research on the subject and wrote a life of St. George, "concluded with giving him entirely up and supposing him only a symbolic device."

It isn't that both the Scots and the English don't have titanic candidates as patron saints. St. Colum Cille, better known as St. Columba, in the thirty-four years from A.D. 563 until his death in A.D. 597, converted the whole of Scotland, a task documented throughout with solid proof. He also founded the royal house of Scotland, putting their first king on the throne of western Argyll. He was an Irishman, born in Ireland.

St. Aidan in A.D. 634 established a monastery on the holy island of Lindisfarne in Northumbria. Operating from this base he built churches, abbeys, and monasteries throughout England, was responsible for the first wholesale conversions to Christianity in that country. He too was an Irishman, born in Ireland.

To throw the accomplishments of these early Irish monks into proper perspective, one should remember that by A.D. 400 all of Europe, including Britain, was overrun by Teutonic tribes from the east and that by A.D. 410 the last Roman legions had been withdrawn from England. "After which withdrawal," to quote from Wells and Barrow, *A Short History of the Roman Empire,* "we have a century of obscurity, of which we know nothing." (Messers Wells and Barrow apparently overlooked Irish history.) It was not until A.D. 597, 165 years after St. Patrick's death, that Pope Gregory the Great sent St. Augustine on the *first papal* mission to England, supposedly because he had been told that the young, blond-haired slaves from Britain, on sale in the Forum, were pagans. This was the same year St. Columba died in his cell at Iona, the tiny island off the west coast of Scotland. It would seem that Gregory—and given the total breakdown of communications throughout Europe, it is not hard to understand why—was unaware that Christianity had been waxing strong in Ireland for 150 years, that it had already conquered Scotland, that St. Aidan had set up his monastery at Lindisfarne seven years earlier, and that the light of Christ was emanating from Ireland all across the Continent, even into the northern part of his own country.

By the time of the Synod of Whitby in A.D. 664, when Roman and Irish monks came to a final showdown in which King Oswy of Northumbria decided in favor of St. Peter, Great Britain had already been Christianized from Ireland. St. Aidan had been dead for thirteen years. No clear picture of these early years can be gained until the fact is squarely faced that the torch carried by St. Patrick was lifted up by Irish monks exclusive of any help from St. Andrew, St.

George, *or* St. Peter. Never have so few achieved so much with so little credit.

Although St. Patrick tried to organize a diocesan church under bishops in Ireland, within a few decades the pastoral nature of the society molded Christianity into a form very close to the Eastern Church. A new and immensely important cultural unit appeared on the Irish scene. With the building of monasteries and abbeys, a sheltered, contemplative existence removed from internecine warfare came into being and in turn helped moderate the passions flaring in the outside world. Chiefs and petty kings who previously had spent a major portion of their time murdering one another now became the principal donors of land and wealth to the creation of the new ecclesiastical sites.

A twofold purpose was served by the erection of these cloistered walls. In the peace available behind them, religion, learning, and education flourished to an extraordinary degree within a relatively short time. It was unique in Europe, attracting scholars from both Britain and the Continent. Schools, universities, and libraries prospered under the sanctity of religion. At the same time the abbeys and monasteries provided something hitherto unknown in Ireland. They became the "cities," the "marketplaces," the centers for arts and crafts in Ireland. They were literally the closest things to towns the Irish had until the Vikings in the ninth century founded the coastal cities. Much of the frustration in modern Ireland results from the fact that this monastic system was first gutted by the Vikings, partially rebuilt by Brian Boru and the Normans, then annihilated forever by the English in the sixteenth and seventeenth centuries. The Irish people are urged to maintain a way of life that has been robbed of its ancient core. It is a bit like asking a population to continue a *sub*urban existence after the urban centers have been removed.

The first towering figure to appear on the Irish monastic scene was St. Finian, "the foster father of the saints of Ireland," who established about A.D. 540 the celebrated school at Clonard. Here the "twelve apostles of Ireland" were educated, and they in turn founded new centers of learning. Within fifty years such sites as Clonmacnoise Lismore, Clonfert, Glendalough, Derry, and Bangor were attracting several thousand students apiece. Twenty-six such schools are still known by name. Saints Ciarnan, Brendan, Carthach, Brigid, and Columba drew up the rules for their own foundations. Not until the twelfth century under the Normans did a single Continental order—Carthusians, Augustinians, Cistercians, Benedictines—enter Ireland. During which time Irish orders were establishing sites throughout Europe. It seems fair to say that the birthplace of the Western monastic system was in Ireland.

At the great school of Armagh one third of the "city" was given over to foreign students. Writing in the seventh century, the Anglo-Saxon Bede, an enthusiastic admirer of the Irish educational system (God, what would he think of the present setup!), described "how certain of the nobles of Britain resorted to the Irish schools and were provided with food and clothes, as well as learning, without expense to themselves." A backhanded compliment to

Irish scholarship is preserved in an eighth-century letter sent by Aldhelm, bishop of Sherborne, to a fellow countryman just home from Ireland: "Why should Ireland pride herself so highly that thither students from England should stream in crowds, just as if Greek and Latin teachers were not to be found upon England's fruitful soil, and to solve the most serious religious problems and to train scholars eager for knowledge?"

What Aldhelm failed to mention was that most of these teachers received their own education in Ireland. By the middle of the seventh century, Hebrew, Latin, and Greek were taught in some Irish schools. Sedulius, one of the great ninth-century Irish scholars, wrote a Greek Psalter which still survives. Both Cormac's Glossary, with place names derived from Greek roots, and the Book of Armagh, with the Lord's Prayer written in Greek characters, bear further tangible witness to Irish classical learning. Nor was the native language overlooked, although some of the clergy wrote contemptuously of the *lingua Scottica vilis*. The bards and wandering monks began to write Irish poetry in meters based on Latin hymns, while others compiled the ancient laws and recorded ancient Irish history in Irish.

Of all the monks St. Columba combined within himself the four great elements of the period: a deep love of the poetry and folklore of the pagan past, a profound knowledge of the classics, a keen appreciation of the visual arts, and a passionate, eloquent faith in Christianity. He was, in the truest sense, an early Irishman of all seasons, one who would gape open-mouthed at certain aspects of the present-day Irish scene.

In 1963, on the fifteen-hundredth anniversary of St. Columba's initial voyage to Iona, the Protestant Church of Ireland, an offshoot of the Protestant Church of England, celebrated the event by building a replica of his open boat and sailed it across the Irish Sea. The Roman Catholic hierarchy passed over the occasion in lofty silence. In 1966 a group of British archaeologists unearthed at Iona the cell in which the saint slept on a flat rock. The way things are going, poor Colum Cille is going to end up a Protestant. What the Knights of Columbus, many of whom believe their founder was Christopher Columbus, will think of all this is a moot question.

St. Columban, like St. Columba, was both a saint and a poet, the author of a book of psalms as well as a number of poems which were set to music. Born in Leinster, he was educated at Bangor in County Down, as were St. Malachi, Johannes Erigena, and a number of monks who worked mainly on the Continent. Bede describes Bangor as divided into seven parts each with a leader and no part containing fewer than three hundred students. The institution was self-supporting, with teachers and scholars doing the manual work themselves.

When Columban and a group of companions crossed over to France in 590 on the first Irish continental mission, they entered literally into a jungle as far as Christianity was concerned, a jungle that had existed for nearly two hundred years. The first monastery founded by Columban was at Château Angeray.

As the number of converts rapidly increased, the great center at Luxeuil was established, and from these two parent institutions new sites sprang up in all directions as had happened in Ireland and Britain. Before long there were over forty ecclesiastical centers which had stemmed directly out of St. Patrick's work in Ireland. From Luxeuil the hardy Columban and a few disciples headed eastward to the Rhine, rowed upriver to Lake Constance where for some time they lived as fishermen, preaching among the Swiss. In 613 Columban proceeded on foot through the Alps to the court of the Lombard princess Theodelinda at Pavia. Here he founded one of the most famous monasteries of Europe, Bobbio, at the base of the Apennines.

Another Irishman, Gallus, who had accompanied Columban in all his previous wanderings, stayed north of the Alps because of illness, and shortly after established in the lonely Steinach Valley the monastery of St. Gall, "the Iona of Germany." St. Gall became the most renowned of all the Irish sites on the Continent and the one most popular with the Irish monks. In the ninth century it was especially noted for its learning and art under the abbot Moengal.

During the seventh century other Irish monks continued on into the Frankish kingdom, establishing mission stations as they went. Among their converts were Franks and Germans, who in turn went out and spread the word of Christ until by the beginning of the eighth century there was an unbroken chain of settlements which stretched from the mouths of the Maas and Rhine rivers in the north to the Rhone valley, the Alps and northern Italy in the south. Nor did they stop at the Rhine. According to Jonas of Bobbio, missionaries from Luxeuil in 620, about the same year Columban founded Bobbio, made their way into Bavaria and later that century Kilian and two Irish companions suffered martyrdom at Würzburg on the Main River. Kilian is still the patron saint of the city of Würzburg.

Patrick must also be credited with the early conversions among both the Frisians and the Saxons. Although the missionaries Victberct, Wilibrord, and the two Hewalds were Englishmen, Bede states that they all received their theological education in Ireland. The great English scholar Alcuin, who taught at the court of Charlemagne and was himself a student at Clonmacnoise, wrote that Wilibrord, the chief apostle of the Frisians, "passed twelve years under celebrated teachers in Ireland."

The names of Irishmen appear everywhere among the monastic records of those centuries. As one broods over such figures as Cataldus of Taranto, Kilian of Franconia, Colman of Lower Austria, St. Donatus of Fiesole, St. Fergil or Virgilius of Salzburg—all Irishmen born in Ireland—and glances over the roll call of such world-famous cities as Poitiers, Metz, Lucca, Verona, Liége, Cologne, Mainz, Münster, Vienna, all listed as "ecclesiastical sites associated with the Irish, fifth to twelfth century"—not to mention those Christian centers founded in Britain and on lonely islands in the north Atlantic—one can only repeat:

Never have so few achieved so much with so little credit.

Their numbers increased with the passing of the years, until in the ninth century we find Eric of Auxerre writing in a letter to Charles the Bald, royal patron and humble student of Johannes Erigena: "What shall I say of Ireland, who, despising the dangers of the deep, is migrating with almost her whole train of philosophers to our coasts?" Montalembert, the historian, wrote that the distinctive quality of the Irish monks, as of the entire nation, was "the imperious necessity of spreading themselves without, of seeking or carrying knowledge and faith afar, and of penetrating into the more distant regions to combat paganism," and he speaks further of their "passion for pilgrimage and preaching."

Few of these dedicated wanderers ever saw their beloved homeland again. What is known of them has been found mostly in Continental records. Their bizarre appearance caused great surprise when they first moved across Europe. Traveling in small bands "they wore a coarse outer woolen garment, in color as it came from the fleece, and under this a white tunic of finer stuff. They were tonsured bare on the front of the head, while the long hair behind flowed down on the back, and the eyelids were painted or stained black." They must have looked much like the figures in early Byzantine art.

"Each had a long, stout *cambutta*, or walking stick, and slung from the shoulder a leathern bottle for water, and a wallet containing his greatest treasure—a book or two and some relics. They spoke a strange language among themselves, used Latin to those who understood it, and made use of an interpreter when preaching. But when they settled down for any length of time they learned and used the native dialect."

Only a handful of the great early Irish scholars can be mentioned here. The breadth of their learning reflects the curricula of the schools in Ireland. A number of these centers offered a twelve-year series of courses which included biblical study, theology, Latin and Greek classics, Gaelic grammar and literature, both poetry and prose, mathematics and astronomy, medicine and law, history and music. Three distinct types of Irish music developed during this period. Among those prominent for their knowledge of both theology and science was St. Fergil, who after serving as abbot of Aghaboe in County Leix, went as bishop in 745 to Salzburg where Pepin, later King of France, entertained him as a guest in his palace for two years.

Fergil was the first person since the ancient Greeks to teach publicly that the earth was round. The Englishman Winifred, later St. Boniface, who had begun to collect converts under the aegis of Rome, wrote letters to Pope Zachary complaining that the bishop of Salzburg had heretically stated people lived on the other side of the earth at the Antipodes. Fergil had already successfully appealed to Zachary in an argument with Boniface over the sacrament of baptism, and the Pope refused to condemn him for his highly unorthodox views on the shape of the earth.

Another Irish monk, Dicuil, wrote in 825 one of the first major works on geography, the finest since classical times, *De mensura orbis terrae*, in which he tells of conversing thirty years earlier with monks who had been in what could only have been Iceland. This work was published during the eighteenth century in both German and French. Contemporary to

Dicuil was a recluse monk, Dungal, the most brilliant astronomer in France during the reign of Charlemagne. The emperor chose him to explain how two solar eclipses might have occurred during the year 810. His reply, *The Epistle of Dungal the Recluse to Charlemagne, Regarding Two Solar Eclipses,* is extant. Thomas Moore wrote of it: "Both in his admission that two solar eclipses could take place within the same year, and his doubt that such a rare incident had occurred in 810 he is equally correct."

In 811 Dungal settled at Pavia and "became a celebrated teacher, drawing pupils from all the surrounding cities." Like Fergil he also "wrote learnedly on ecclesiastical subjects." He is believed to have brought to Italy the early seventh-century *Antiphonary* of St. Congall's monastery in Bangor, one of many priceless Irish manuscripts taken to the Continent to avoid destruction by the Danes. After lying neglected for a thousand years it was discovered at Bobbio by the Italian scholar Muratori, who published it in the eighteenth century. Others have turned up all over Europe, today are scattered through the museums and libraries of the world. How many were destroyed or have disappeared can only be estimated by the number of ecclesiastical centers which were sacked and burned in Ireland.

The discovery in the last century by M. D'Arbois de Jubainville in the library at Nancy of a collection of Irish glosses written on a single leaf within a manuscript cover reveals the meticulousness with which the ancient Irish studied chronology and astronomical phenomena. The entries, a proposed table of contents for a treatise on the calendar, were interpreted by M. Henri Gaidoz and published by de Jubainville, who assigned them to the ninth century. That this knowledge of astronomy and mathematics extended back into prehistoric times is apparent from the wealth of evidence which has been sifted out by scholars from Irish mythology.

The most famous graduate of Clonmacnoise was Alcuin of York, a Saxon whose role in the eighth-century educational history of France was monumental. At Charlemagne's request Alcuin set up a palace school which was both a study and a workshop for the translation and copying of ancient manuscripts. Its influence was felt throughout the entire realm. Among Alcuin's pupils were Charlemagne, his wife Hildegarde, his sons and daughter Gisela.

Here one sees a tightly knit, "international" group transforming the intellectual, cultural, and artistic face of Europe. A German-born monarch whose father, Pepin, had already found his chief inspiration in the Irish-born bishop of Salzburg, St. Fergil, employs a Saxon monk, educated in Ireland, to help him carry on his duties as King of France and Emperor of the Holy Roman Empire.

Perhaps the most important evidence of the extent of Irish influence in Europe during this period is found in the correspondence of Alcuin with Colcu the Wise, chief professor at Clonmacnoise. Colcu was considered "the wisest of all men" at the end of the eighth century and a lovely prayer in Irish by him still exists. Alcuin refers to him as "most holy father," calls himself "his son," and sends him presents for charitable purposes, some from himself, some from Charlemagne. Situated on a broad, sweeping bend of the upper Shannon, Clonmacnoise was for many years a disgraceful morass, shattered by Vikings and English. It was finally rescued in 1960 through the sole efforts of a local parish priest, Father Frank O'Donoghue, now dead, and turned over to the National Monuments Trust, but innumerable other sites lie neglected and abandoned.

It was during the second half of the ninth century, as the Viking onslaughts increased in fury, that scholars from Clonmacnoise, Bangor, and elsewhere in Ireland reached their peak of renown. At Liége a group of brilliant monks—Fergus, Blandus, Marcus, Dubthach, and Beuchell—were gathered around their celebrated leader, Sedulius Scotus, whose Greek Psalter has already been mentioned. The correspondence of the Liége group is full of references to Ireland, some of their works on grammar and philosophy were apparently written in Ireland, and in one poem Sedulius himself offers up thanks for a victory by the Irish over the Vikings.

At the court in Laon of Charles the Bald, grandson of Charlemagne, the most distinguished Irish scholar of all times, Johannes Scotus Erigena, held undisputed sway. *The Cambridge Medieval History* refers to Erigena as "the Irish genius . . . the first great figure in medieval philosophy," and terms his major work, *De divisione naturae*, "one of the most remarkable books of the world. . . . Dark centuries succeeded John the Scot, yet in them were preserved the ideas and the literary implements which accompanied the reawakening." (*Scotus* or *Scottus* was the original Latin name for *Irishman.*)

The last great Irish scholar who belongs rightfully

to this period won his first great reputation at Oxford. Duns Scotus, a member of the Francisan order, became a fellow of Merton College. It was said that within a short time over thirty thousand students were attracted there because of his lectures. "His fame was now become so universal, that the general of his order commanded him to go to Paris, that the students of that university might also profit from his lectures." He went to Paris at the age of thirty-nine and within three years was appointed regent of the university. The following year he was sent to Cologne where "he was received with great pomp and ceremony by the magistrates and nobles of that city." Unfortunately he died suddenly at the age of forty-three. His works composing twelve folio volumes were published at Lyons in 1639 by Luke Wadding, the great Irish Franciscan scholar. He was considered the equal in knowledge, though not in originality, of Johannes Erigena, of whose work six volumes have been published with a score more manuscripts preserved.

One of the most extraordinary aspects of Ireland's golden age was the speed with which learning and missionary activities moved ahead after the conversion of the race to Christianity. By comparison the rebirth of Irish visual art, the last phenomenon in this incredible period, took a bit longer. Not until well into the seventh century did it come into full bloom. Then one finds in three closely related phases strong traces of the creative imagination and expert craftsmanship of the prehistoric past blended with brand-new techniques and fresh inspiration which sprang from the infused element of Christianity. There was, however, a connecting bridge between intellectual development and visual expression in the illuminated manuscripts.

The oldest known manuscript is *The Cathach of St. Columba* which may well have been done in that saint's lifetime. Already the Irish had developed an original script style and their own unique approach to ornamentation. By the early seventh century a far more exciting invention had taken place, the so-called Carpet Page, where an entire sheet was given over to an intricate, abstract labyrinth of rosettes, spirals, and crosses, painted in brilliant yellow, blue, dark green, and red. The first monumental work was the *Book of Durrow* from the late seventh century which, with the *Book of Kells*, is in the Trinity College (Dublin) Library.

While these manuscripts were an integral part of literary development, they pointed the way toward exquisite related work in gold, silver, and bronze, supplemented by a highly skillful use of enamel and what is called millefiori, tiny colored bits floating within the enamel or set in panels, really a sort of mosaic. Both abstract and representational work in these objects parallel closely the artistry of the illuminated manuscripts, and as more than one authority has pointed out, the same intricate patterns underlie the literature and philosophy of the period.

Most difficult of all to comprehend, as far as the twentieth-century mind is concerned, is the fabulous Book of Kells. "As coherently detailed as life, with every minute cell of its organic structure carefully composed," it provides one of the recurring, obsessive themes of Joyce's *Finnegans Wake*. If we could understand *Finnegans Wake*, we might better understand the Irish and the labyrinth of their ancient past. And vice versa.

With abbeys and monasteries prospering, most of the gold, silver, and bronze work was concerned with ecclesiastical objects—chalices, bowls, crosses, "shrines" for precious books and relics, including the croziers, curved in the shape of the walking sticks of saintly leaders which they enclosed. There were other purely ornamental secular objects—brooches, badges, buckles, and the like. In both groups masterpieces were created which had no equals anywhere in Europe. Like the illuminated manuscripts they too are found today scattered through the museums of the world, many in Scandinavia where they have been excavated from Viking graves, booty brought home from the bloody raids.

Some of the finest objects are in Dublin's National Museum, including what are considered the best single examples from each group, secular and ecclesiastical, the Tara Brooch from Bettystown, County Meath, and the Ardagh Chalice from County Limerick.

Words fail to capture the soaring spirit of the Tara Brooch and the Ardagh Chalice. The brooch is of bronze with amber, amethyst, enamel and gold filigree ornamentation, the chalice of silver with panels and handles, a dazzling array of gold filigree, bronze, and enamel. As one wanders from the prehistoric displays to these Christian pieces, it is difficult to conceive of them as anything but intrinsic parts of one continuing, though interrupted, tradition.

As in the case of the illuminated manuscripts, the influence of the Irish metalwork on subsequent European art was enormous. The entire Urnes style in Scandinavia, named after a particular carved wooden church in Norway, found its original inspiration in the subtly interwoven animal designs on pieces plundered from Ireland during the ninth century. In the Irish work one sees numerous forerunners of details which later turn up in Gothic architectural design.

The third visual medium, over and above the illuminated manuscripts and the metalwork, was peculiar to Ireland alone, the great stone high crosses. Here the same abstract intricacies found in the manuscripts and in the gold, silver, and bronze objects were translated into sandstone and in the Barrow Valley, probably at an earlier date, into granite. Each medium allowed for special scope of imagination and expression, called for different techniques, but the underlying themes were always the same. At first abstract designs were used exclusively on the upright shafts, with animals and human beings confined to the bases, but these were soon moved up onto the shafts themselves. Eventually a whole new type of art came into being, with particular emphasis on biblical scenes. A use of the flat, vertical surfaces evolved, somewhat similar to the carved scenes on Roman victory arches which found their ultimate expression during the Renaissance in Ghiberti's immortal bronze doors at the baptistery in Florence.

So much superb written and photographic material has been published dealing with early Irish visual art, so much can be seen in museums, there is no point in going over more of the same ground. Nor is there room unfortunately to tackle the mystery of Ireland's

Round Towers, some eighty of which still exist. In their mathematical precision, astronomical significance, and phallic symbolism, they raise questions which have never been satisfactorily answered. In fact, in the face of arbitrary decisions that they were erected as refuges from the Danes and/or as watchtowers, it has been some time since the right questions have been asked. Firsthand examination will convince the open-minded observer that they could hardly have been designed as watchtowers—most of them are situated in hollows—nor as places of refuge. To fire-bearing scavengers like the Vikings, they would have served as handy ovens for instant roasting. They do contradict the flat statement one finds in countless books that the Irish didn't know how to build in stone until the Normans taught them how. It is now universally agreed they were built at least two centuries before the arrival of the Normans.

As one surveys Ireland during those long-departed centuries, it seems fair to say that in literature, in the blending together of three distinct but closely related visual art forms, in music, in science, theology, and philosophy, in general learning including a broad knowledge of the classics, and above all in their ability to blend a deep joy for the world around them with intense *spiritual*, not *churchly*, fervor, an inner ecstasy which sent them rushing off to spread the word of God to other people—the Irish enjoyed a position unrivaled in the Western world.

Surveying the modern scene, contemplating the present sorry state of the arts, one can only despair that the Irish will ever again, in their homeland, attain to such glorious heights.

*I am not writing Irish history at the behest of anyone or with any hope of profiting by it, but because I thought that a country as worthy of honour as Ireland and people as noble as those who have inhabited it, should not go down into oblivion till their story was told. And I think my estimate of the Irish should be accepted, because it is mainly of the Gaels that I treat. If anyone thinks that I am predisposed in their favour, let him recollect that I am not likely to praise them beyond their deserts because I belong myself to the Anglo-Irish.*

—Geoffrey Keating, *Groundwork of the Knowledge of Ireland* (1632)

The English are a remarkable race! At any given period in their history, no matter what course the majority was following, a fairly large minority would be fighting along completely different lines, motivated solely by their own uncompromising personal standards of fair play and justice.

This ever-changing but ever-present minority created a monumental history of the English which unfolded concurrent to the less noble thoughts and actions of their contemporaries, influenced profoundly not so much those around them but those who came after them in their own country, as well as a large portion of the world's population, and in the end played a key role in the eventual freeing of subject nations all the way from Ireland to India. Most of the philosophical concepts which motivated the Young Irelanders sprang from English sources, and it would appear that only through a reawareness of these concepts will the Irish work out successfully their eventual destiny. It is this dual nature of English history that makes it possible to be motivated by Anglo-Saxon ideals and at the same time thoroughly detest everything the English did or tried to do to the Irish and what they are still trying to do north of the border.

Geoffrey Keating, whose *Forus Feasa,* the first general history of Ireland written in Irish, was widely and illegally circulated in manuscript copies, was the front runner for a number of English and Anglo-Irish scholars who during the last three centuries have tried to paint an objective picture of the Irish. One thinks of Lord Chesterfield's pithy comment on eighteenth-century Ireland which as viceroy he knew so well: "If the military forces had shot half as many landlords as it had Whiteboys, it would have done more to restore quiet." Of Sir John Norris, who was convinced there were fewer "idiots and cowards" in Ireland than in any other country. And Sir Henry

Bourgchier, the fifth Earl of Bath, who in the same year that Keating's work appeared, wrote: "No people is more in awe of their sovereign, or more willing or cordial to obey when justice is duly ministered to them, their wrongs redressed, the oppressors and offenders punished according to their deserts." One could compile an imposing bedside handbook to be distributed on the next Twelfth of July to all loyal members of the Orange Order, composed entirely of laudatory remarks made by Anglo-Saxons about the native Irish.

Unfortunately those voices were shouting into the teeth of a mounting gale. The downbeat which had been administered to the Irish since the Norman invasions by Giraldus Cambrensis, Stanihurst, Campion, and the rest was stepped up in volume and tempo after the battle of Kinsale, to such a degree that by the beginning of the twentieth century the mass of semiliterate and illiterate people in England, on the Continent, in the United States, and even in Ireland had come to believe that by nature the Irish were suitable only for duty as housemaids, coachmen, cooks, bartenders, and manual laborers. In short, their sorrows stemmed directly out of their own failings. Almost every pseudoscientific argument today directed against the Negroes—brain capacity, reflex actions, inherent racial traits—have in their day been directed against the Irish, a fact which a large percentage of half-educated, extremely vocal, reactionary Irish-Americans don't seem to realize. The grouping of Kikes, Katholics, and Koons together was no accident.

One has only to thumb through nineteenth-century

copies of *Punch* and *The Illustrated London News* or *Harper's Weekly* to trace the development of Pat and Mike, of the stubble-chinned, pug-nosed, squint-eyed creatures dressed in cast-off top hats and tail coats, clay pipes cocked at a jaunty angle, resembling baboons and monkeys more than human beings, who found their counterparts on the stage of every music hall, vaudeville and burlesque house in the English-speaking world, their coat of arms the potato and the pig. Later they emerged in American comic strips as Jiggs and Maggie, Moon Mullins, and Happy Hooligan, and are still given a systematic going over by the BBC in such gay little ditties as "Rafferty's Motor Car," "Paddy McGinty's Goat," and "Seven Nights Drunk," which have as much to do with life in Ireland as they do with life on Mars. As for the shillelagh-and-shamrock stage Irishman with his "top o' the marnin" and "the back o' me hand to ye," his "begorrys" and "bedads," he must have gone out of fashion along with Charles Lever. He is certainly absent from the Irish scene today.

One of the surviving idiocies in the United Kingsom and in Ireland is the practice common on both sides of the Irish Sea to emphasize in every possible fashion the underlying racial differences between the "Anglo-Saxons" and "the Celts." In actual fact the pre-Celtic "forgotten" strain is probably dominant in both islands.

Complicating this mumbo jumbo even further is the fact that between the ninth century and the fatal sixteenth century the two races that conquered England—the Scandinavians (popularly referred to as Danes or Vikings) and the Normans—entered Ireland in great numbers and in a reverse twist to what happened in England were conquered or absorbed by the Irish. One has only to reflect on the prominent "Irish" names of Norman origin—Fitzgerald, Burke, Barry, Roach, Dillon, Prendergast, Fitzpatrick, Costello, McQuillan, Daly, Coogan, Delaney, and scores more—to appreciate the fact that there is almost as much Norman as pre-Norman blood in Ireland. While the Danes stayed more in the fortified seaports and were less homogenized with the Irish, most of the Normans who came to Ireland were already partially Celtic through their intermarriages with the Welsh. They strengthened the dispersed pattern of the Irish way of life by spreading themselves thinly out across the island and intermarried with the native Irish to such a degree that it is safe to say today that practically everyone in Ireland is part Norman. (Of the ten farmers who live nearest to us in County Limerick, six bear Norman names.) An interesting case in point was the late President Kennedy —Norman on his maternal Fitzgerald side, native on his paternal side. A Kennedy, or Cenneidigh, became King of Munster in A.D. 954 and was the father of the immortal Brian Boru.

Added to the Norman and Danish strains were a large number of Old English families who as already mentioned remained Roman Catholic during the sixteenth century and were swept off their lands and into the common Irish melting pot during the Cromwellian settlement. Long before the Tudor monarchs began their systematic reduction of Ireland, as early as the mid-fourteenth century with the enactment of the Statutes of Kilkenny, the Crown abandoned any attempts to bring the great Norman families scattered through the country back into the fold. They had become "more Irish than the Irish," offering far more opposition to the British government than the native Irish. The Statutes of Kilkenny were designed solely to maintain a bridgehead within the Pale around Dublin from which a later attempt to conquer the island could be launched.

No single fact attests to the unique indestructibility of the Irish than that, after 739 years of attempts by the Danes and Normans to conquer them, in 1534 the Crown, out of some 32,000 square miles, was in effective control of only four hundred square miles, around Dublin and extending for a short distance into County Kildare. Augustin Thierry, "the father of modern history," termed the period "one of unconquerable obstinacy, perhaps the greatest example a people has ever given."

Now it so happens that I have held aside until this late date what I believe is the finest example of all as to what the Irish can accomplish when freed of the shackles that still bind them in their homeland. As might be expected, it is the least known and appreciated chapter in Irish history. It has to do with those Irishmen who fled the country during the seventeenth and eighteenth centuries, before the great mass migrations of the nineteenth century began.

Lecky, the great Anglo-Irish Protestant historian whose statue today dominates the campus of Trinity College, Dublin, wrote of "how large a portion of the energy and ability was employed in foreign lands, and how ruinous must have been the consequences at home."

Jonathan Swift, noblest of all eighteenth-century Irish minds saluted "those gentlemen of Ireland, who, with all the disadvantages of being exiles and strangers, have been able to distinguish themselves, in so many parts of Europe, by their valor and conduct above all other nations."

It should be remembered that this phase of Irish history was being enacted at the same time that the Roman Catholics in Ireland, the brothers and sisters, fathers and mothers, cousins and neighbors of these men overseas, were being shoved down into poverty and obscurity, and while the Irish Protestants were making their own desperate, unsuccessful attempt to win independence from the English. What follows indicates the kind of civilization the Irish could build in Ireland if they were given half a chance, if they could only regain full possession of their bodies and souls.

Unfortunately the material for this phase of Irish history has never been completely assembled, although research is in progress on a number of fronts. The enormity of the task is well illustrated by Thomas Carlyle's comment while he was engaged in writing his *History of Frederick the Great*. He tells of continually running across in Prussia the names of "very many Irish; and there is not the least distinct account of any of them."

"The Flight of the Wild Geese," after the treaty of Limerick in 1691, is only part of the story. Throughout the preceding century, stepping up greatly after the Cromwellian settlement, a steady stream flowed out of Ireland, and after Limerick the stream turned into a torrent. According to calculations made by the

War Office of the Irish Republic, during the fifty-four years from 1691 to the battle of Fontenoy in 1745, over 400,000 Irishmen died in the French armed services. M. de la Pouce, the French military historian, estimated on the basis of research conducted in the archives of the War Department in Paris, that during the 150 years from 1650 to 1800 "more than 750,000 Irishmen gave their lives for the glory of France." Taking each country in turn, here are just the barest details of what happened:

In France Viscount Mountcashel, Justin MacCarthy, who led five thousand crack troops abroad before the battle of the Boyne, became the first commander of the Irish Brigade in the service of Louis XIV. Fighting what they felt was a continuation of the struggle against England, MacCarthy and his men were engaged in a number of fierce battles along the Rhine and in Savoy, Mountcashel dying in 1694 of wounds received in action.

The O'Briens proved worthy descendants of Brian Boru and, atoning for the sins committed by some of the family in Ireland, covered themselves with particular glory. Charles O'Brien, the sixth Lord Clare and Earl of Thomond, born during the siege of Limerick, became a marshal of France, commanding the Irish Brigade at Fontenoy. His uncle was killed fighting for the French cause at Marsaglia in 1693, his father perished at Ramillies in 1706.

At Fontenoy the Duke of Cumberland, younger son of King George II, had hacked his way with fifteen thousand troops through the heart of the French Army. Twice Marshal Saxe had urged retreat. With the battle apparently lost, fifteen Irish regiments held in reserve under Charles O'Brien stormed down the slope of St. Antoine Hill, shouting their battle cry, "Remember Limerick!" They struck full blast and shattered the English forces who fled the battlefield leaving over eight thousand dead and wounded. Ninety-eight Irish officers were killed in the engagement but O'Brien, although in the thickest of the action, survived.

When King George received news of Fontenoy, he is said to have exclaimed, "Curse the laws that deprive me of such subjects!" (Among the "privileges" denied the Irish at that time was the right to serve in the English Army or Navy.) King George offered to restore to Charles O'Brien, if he would change his religion and allegiance, his titles and estates in Ireland which amounted to more than eighty thousand acres. O'Brien refused.

On the battlefield that day at Fontenoy King Louis XV raised Count Thomas de Lally for his exceptional courage to the rank of brigadier general. The French barons de Tollendal are descended from Thomas de Lally, "Tollendal" being a free translation of *Tullagh-na-Daly*, "Daly's Hill," in Galway, which bears out in turn that the Irish name Daly is a corruption of the original Norman name de Lally. King Louis the next day came and thanked in person each of the Irish corps, handing out a large number of promotions and pensions.

Peter, Count Lacy, won supreme honors. Born in the peaceful hamlet of Ballingarry in County Limerick, one of the Wild Geese, he first enlisted in the French Army, then continued to Russia where he became a field marshal, serving both Peter the Great and

Catherine the Great. He completely reorganized the Russian Army, for fifty years fought in every campaign against all comers including the Swedes, Turks, and Poles. With him in Russia were a number of other Irish officers, including a Commander Count O'Rourke. This same Lacy family provided a field marshal to the Austro-Hungarian Empire and a general to Spain, the latter becoming ambassador to Russia and Sweden.

Fox-hunting in the glorious country around Ballingarry, I took time out to inquire if any De Lacys or Lacys still lived in the area. They have all disappeared, but the ruins of their castle still stand and forty-five families bearing the name are listed in the 1967 Irish telephone directory, scattered throughout the Republic.

Among the Irishmen serving France during this century one of the Dillons (again a prominent Norman family) whose exploits became legendary was created a marshal of France, while another became bishop of Toulouse. Richard Cusack was also a marshal of France. One of the O'Maras was a brigadier general, while a Talbot became the French ambassador at the court of Frederick the Great. Henry James Clarke had a particularly distinguished career. A marshal of France, he was appointed minister of war by Napoleon, serving during the vital years from 1807 to 1814. He took over the governorship of Vienna in 1805 from an Irishman in the service of Austria, Count Andrew O'Reilly. In 1814 Clarke was created the Duc de Feltre.

Another crucial early battle in which the Irish were credited with turning certain defeat into French victory took place in 1702 at Cremona in Italy. The Austrians under Prince Eugene stole in during the night by an unguarded passage, seized Marshal de Villeroi, the French commander, and had gained almost full possession of the city when six hundred Irishmen under General Dillon tumbled out of bed and fought in their nightshirts hand-to-hand through the streets and in and out of the houses until the Austrians were finally driven off, leaving two thousand dead behind. Two hundred and twenty-three of the Irish were killed. They are still referred to in that part of Italy as "the men who fought in their nightshirts."

Charles Forman, another objective English historian, in his *A Defense of the Courage, Honour, and Loyalty of the Irish Nation*, published in 1754, "in answer to the Scandalous Reflections in the Free-Briton and others," wrote of the trust Louis XIV placed in the Irish—in Flanders, Alsace, Piedmont, Catalonia, "in every place where the War was hottest . . . they have never made the least false step, or have had the least Blot on their Scutcheon."

Vendôme showed them a lifelong "Esteem and Notice" for their "Courage and the Intrepidity of their Behaviour" at the siege of Barcelona, where Dillon again distinguished himself, as he also did in the successful defense of the great Vendôme-designed fortress at Toulon.

In 1792, on the eve of the French Revolution, the Irish Brigade was finally dissolved. The doomed Louis XVI presented in person to the members of the brigade a new standard, on which a golden harp was entwined with both shamrocks and fleurs-de-lis. Inscribed was the legend: "1692–1792 *Semper et*

*Ubique Fidelis.*" But the Irish role in France did not end with the Revolution. Henry James Clarke has already been mentioned. During the 1848 insurrection the French minister of war was General Louis Eugène Cavaignac, a Wild Geese descendant of the Kavenaughs (née MacMurroughs) from Leinster. Cavaignac was the popular candidate for the presidency against Napoleon III, receiving 1.5 million votes to 5.5 million for the future emperor.

In the next decade another Franco-Irishman bearing a name first encountered in County Monaghan attained worldwide prominence. Marie Edme Patrice Maurice de MacMahon, after his decisive victory in the war with Austria, was created Duc de Magenta and marshal of France. He commanded the French forces in the war with Prussia and became the first president of the Republic in 1873. At this stage in European history the destinies of a large portion of the Continental population rested in Irish hands. MacMahon was the head of state in France. Count Taaffe of Roscommon between 1868 and 1893 was twice premier of the Austro-Hungarian Empire. (The Taaffes were originally from County Meath, of Norman extraction.) The prime minister of Spain was Leopold O'Donnell, the first Duke of Tetuan, descended from the great Hugh O'Donnell. He had commanded the Spanish forces in the conquest of Morocco. (His son, Charles O'Donnell, the Duke of Tetuan, was also prime minister of Spain several times in the twentieth century.)

Finishing off this résumé of the Irish in France, Aristide Briand, eleven times premier of France, was the great grandson of another of the Wild Geese, Conal O'Brien. (General Álvaro Obregón, president of Mexico in the twenties, was also a wandering member of the O'Brien family.) On his paternal side General Charles de Gaulle is partly Irish, descended from the ancient MacCartan tribe of Cork. His great-grandfather married Josephine MacCartan, and their daughter, Josephine de Gaulle, wrote and published a life of Daniel O'Connell.

Turning next to Spain, for nine years from 1754 to 1763, Richard Wall, whose parents were both born in Waterford, was prime minister of that country, having previously served as ambassador to England. Patrick Lawless held the same post in 1714. Lieutenant-General Don Carlos Felix O'Neill, son of Sir Neil O'Neill, who was killed in the battle of the Boyne, became a great favorite of Charles III. For many years he was governor of Havana, dying in Madrid in 1791, aged 110. In 1799 Field Marshal Arturo O'Neile was appointed governor of Yucatan, commanding the fleet which attacked Honduras. In the same year General Gonzales O'Farrel was ambassador to Berlin and in 1808 became Spanish minister of war. Don Pedro O'Daly was governor of Rosas in 1800, while General John O'Donoghue, who was Spanish chief of staff during the Peninsular Campaign, died in 1816 as viceroy of Mexico.

Field Marshal Alexander Count O'Reilly, a cousin of the Viennese governor, Andrew Count O'Reilly, served with great distinction in three European armies. Born in Ireland in the early eighteenth century, O'Reilly saved Charles III's life during a revolt in Madrid. He reformed the Spanish Army and became its commander-in-chief, fought for Charles IV during the War of Spanish Succession in Italy, where he was lamed for life. He served in the Austrian Army in the campaign against the Prussians, then enlisted under Louis XV and for his services to France was appointed lieutenant general of Louisiana.

Ambrosio O'Higgins, the Marqués de Osorno, was born in Ireland in 1720. He was viceroy of Peru under Ferdinand VI, Charles III, and Charles IV, during which time he conquered all of Chile and Peru. He was still active as viceroy when he died in 1801. His son, Bernardo O'Higgins, undid much of his work but added immortality to the name O'Higgins. He led the struggle for Chilean independence from 1810 to 1817, was the head of the first permanent national government from 1817 to 1823, and today is known as the liberator of Chile. Many of the families bearing Irish names in South America first established their roots in that country during the era of the two O'Higgins.

When one turns to the eighteenth century in Vienna, the capital of the Austro-Hungarian Empire, there are so many Irishmen on the scene it is difficult to know where to start. Nine field marshals of the imperial army were either born in Ireland or had parents who were born there. Three members of the O'Donnell family received the Grand Cross of the Order of Maria Theresa, comparable to the Victoria Cross or the Congressional Medal of Honor, awarded by members of the order.

*The Annual Register* (London) affords a revealing glimpse of what occurred at the Austrian court on St. Patrick's Day in the year 1767.

> On the 17th of this month [March] his Excellency, Count Mahony, Ambassador from Spain to the Court of Vienna, gave a grand entertainment in honour of St. Patrick, to which were invited all persons of condition, that were of Irish descent; being himself a descendant of an illustrious family of that kingdom. Among many others were present Count Lacy, President of the Council of War, the Generals O'Donnell, McGuire, O'Kelly, Browne, Plunkett, and McEligot, four Chiefs of the Grand Cross, two Governors, several Knights Military, six Staff Officers, four Privy Councillors; with the principal officers of state, who, to shew their respect to the Irish nation, wore crosses in honour of the same, as did the whole Court.

Of the group mentioned, Count Lacy was Field Marshal Francis Maurice Lacy of the same Ballingarry family as Peter Lacy. After many active years in the field this adopted son of Austria served from 1766 to 1778 as war minister and president of the war council.

Browne was Field Marshal Maximilian Ulysses von Browne, born in 1705 of Irish parents. He fought in Silesia against Frederick the Great, who often referred to him as "his teacher in the art of war." Appointed governor of Transylvania, Browne was colonel-in-chief of the 36th Bohemian Infantry which continued to bear his name until the Czechoslovakian Republic was founded in 1918. Another Browne, a cousin, became a field marshal in the Russian Army and governor of Riga.

McGuire was General Count John Sigismund Maguire, formerly of County Fermanagh. A worthy descendant of the valiant Hugh Maguire, he too received the Grand Cross of the Order of Maria Theresa, and was appointed governor of Carinthia.

O'Kelly was General Count William O'Kelly of County Galway. He was commander in chief of the Austrian forces at the battle of Breslau in 1756. One would like to think he sprang from Taig O'Kelly, "the most ardent spirit" serving under Brian Boru at Clontarf.

Plunkett was Lieutenant General Baron Thomas Plunkett, born in Kilkenny in 1716. A kinsman of Lord Dunsany, Plunkett was adjutant general during the War of the Spanish Succession, and became governor of Antwerp.

What is remarkable about these eighteenth-century Irishmen is that throughout Europe they were not only magnificent soldiers, but were also capable of stepping into key diplomatic, political, and administrative positions. There is room for just a few more. General Count James MacDonnell was serving as imperial chamberlain at the time of his death in 1766. He must have lived to a ripe old age, for it was he who at Cremona sixty-four years earlier captured the French Marshal de Villeroi only to have victory snatched from his grasp by Dillon's six hundred men.

Field Marshal Count Francis Taaffe, the third Earl of Carlingford, was born at Ballymote, County Sligo, the family having been evicted from Meath. He brought with him to Vienna a regiment of eighteen hundred Irishmen, became a Knight of the Golden Fleece, governor of Nancy, and prime minister. He was the ancestor of the nineteenth-century chancellor. General Baron Thomas Brady of Cootehill,

County Cavan, became governor of Dalmatia and privy councillor to the Emperor. Colonel William Count von Bourckh was the second son of Walter Gall Burke (from de Burgh to Burke to von Bourckh), one of five brothers whose father lived in County Kilkenny, and who all had outstanding careers in Austria. William was created Baron of Holstein in Silesia.

Three Walshs won high rank for their valor: Field Marshal Francis Wenzil Walsh, Major General Oliver Walsh, who also served as imperial chamberlain, and his son, Field Marshal George Oliver Walsh, Knight of the Polish White Eagle, governor of Messina in Sicily, generalissimo of the Austrian Armies in Turkey. The Walshs came from Carrickmines outside Dublin.

Lastly two Irishmen who fled to Austria before they were twenty, who won what should have been lasting fame but who, like the others, are all but forgotten:

Laval Nugent, born in County Galway, in 1777, entered the Austrian Army at the age of sixteen, became a field marshal in his early thirties, married the Duchess Riario-Sforza, was created a prince of the Holy Roman Empire and a magnate of Hungary.

Philip Magawly, born in County Leix, also rose to the rank of field marshal, was created Count Cerati of Bavaria, and appointed governor of Prague. This was one family which did return to Ireland. The field marshal's great-great-grandson, Colonel Magawly de Calry of the 15th Hussars, was killed fighting for England at the battle of the Somme in 1916. It is typically paradoxical of the Irish that, at the exact moment when they were summoning up their energies for a final showdown with England, over 400,000 Irishmen, one out of every three able-bodied men in Ireland, *volunteered* during the first World War for service in the British armed services!

As one surveys the eighteenth-century scene it becomes apparent that Irishmen occupied key military positions and top administrative posts all the way from Russia and other parts of Eastern Europe, through Austria, Hungary, Germany, the Netherlands, France, Italy, Spain, across to Cuba, Peru, Mexico, and Louisiana. My thoughts turn again to those three young Irish Roman Catholics born within twenty-five miles of one another in Northern Ireland during the last century—Lord Russell of Kilowen, Thomas D'Arcy Mcgee, and Gavan Duffy—and again one can only groan at the amount of youthful talent going to waste in Ireland, North and South at this very moment.

Unfortunately, by the beginning of the nineteenth century, the overwhelming majority of these Irish *émigrés*, who had left Ireland because they refused to live other than free men in their own country, became—through their long, intimate relationship with royalty in the form of absolute monarchy and with the Church of Rome—augmented by their intense distaste for the new liberalism embodied in the American and French Revolutions, more of a hindrance than a help in the fight for Irish independence. They were more afraid of the masses—including the Irish masses—than they were anxious to help set Ireland free.

After the Irish Brigade was dissolved in 1792, a large percentage of its members crossed the Channel and enlisted in the British Army to fight against the French revolutionary forces. Others, like Daniel O'Connell's uncle, the last colonel of the brigade, returned home to Ireland and took seats on the sidelines, moderate or immoderate supporters of "law and order," which in this case meant English law and English order.

This aspect of Irish history explains in large measure why Daniel O'Connell, himself educated in France, funked out when the chips were down, why he publicly proclaimed that "freedom was not worth the shedding of a single drop of blood." Poor O'Connell never really understood what was going on around him. Having won Catholic emancipation with the help of the clergy, he was forever after subtly thwarted by them at every turn in his efforts to repeal the Act of Union.

Even Sir Thomas Wyse, one of O'Connell's most dedicated supporters, wrote within months of the passage of the Catholic Emancipation Act: "No one measure has tended so decidedly to put the seal to the union of the two countries, or to annihilate, or at least retard, all chance and desire of a national separation."

While today the statue of Parnell stands at the top of O'Connell Street and the glorious monument to Wolfe Tone has recently been unveiled in St. Stephen's Green, there are those in Ireland who bitterly hate their memory, not because they were Anglo-Irish, not because they were Protestants, but because each of them waged a desperate fight for the rights of the common people of Ireland.

In a book published some thirty years ago, *The*

*Irish Future*, another descendant of the mighty Hugh O'Donnell, Charles J. O'Donnell, M.P. at Westminster before the Irish Republic was established, characterizes Tone as a "radical and communist," Parnell as a "communist, anarchist, and adulterer." In O'Donnell's opinion, the Protestant landowners in Ireland were "driven into the anti-Irish camp by the communist teachings of Parnell and Michael Davitt." A staunch Roman Catholic and in his own way a passionate Irish patriot, O'Donnell further describes the efforts of those who won his country's freedom as "the outrages committed by Sinn Féin fanatics and criminals."

These are, alas, still the private and semipublic opinions of many highly placed personages in Ireland today, and find frequent expression in the newspaper columns. It is a narrow-minded, partisan, uneducated attitude that finds reflection, as compared to the Kennedy brothers and their supporters, in the political, economic, and social views of such Irish-American rabble-rousers as Father Coughlin and Joe McCarthy. More recently such prominent figures as Mayor Daley of Chicago and former police chief "Bull" O'Connor of Atlanta have come to epitomize the hundreds of transplanted Irishmen who, forgetting the past centuries of oppression in Ireland, are causing their forces to don crash helmets and lift nightsticks against demonstrators in America.

To balance off these headstrong buckos, it seems fitting to end this chapter with the lines written by General Robert E. Lee concerning Meagher's Irish Brigade, which served in the Union Army during the American Civil War. Thomas Francis Meagher was condemned to be hanged, drawn, and quartered for his part in the 1848 Irish uprising. His sentence was commuted, and he escaped to the United States where he attained the rank of brigadier general. His sword and the flags carried by his men at Fredericksburg can be seen today at the City Hall in Waterford. Lee, who commanded the Confederate forces from the ridge to the south of Fredericksburg, wrote of Meagher:

> Though not the equal of Cleburne in military genius, he rivalled him in bravery and in the affections of his soldiers. The gallant stand which his bold Brigade made at Fredericksburg is well known. Never were men so brave. They ennobled their race by their splendid stand on that desperate occasion.

When one remembers what happened in Ireland during the two centuries following the treaty of Limerick, the amazing thing is that *any* Roman Catholic who could walk or crawl stayed in the country. It would seem that those who could get out did get out. And those who did get out wrote such a record it should settle for all time—Pat and Mike, Jiggs and Maggie, Happy Hooligan and Moon Mullins to the contrary—the question of what the Irish can accomplish when given their half a chance.

Before World War II there was a popular saying in Europe that the situation in Germany was serious but not hopeless, while the situation in Austria was hopeless but not serious. There is a general tendency to regard Ireland today in the latter light. "Sure, and what difference is there how the Irish are doing? What's all the fuss about? They're a grand people, and it's a grand old country. It always was and, please God, it always will be!" At which point I should probably apologize to the reader for not dwelling more on the whimsical and the picturesque, the poetic nature, the sparkling wit of the Irish. But as I said before, when a patient is suffering from a lingering disease, it's hard to rhapsodize about his curly hair and fine figure.

It is the popular thing today in Ireland—as well as in England and on the Continent—to think with grim satisfaction of the United States as a "sick" country. Considering the image of America reflected in the press and on television, this is perfectly understandable. I only wish I could take several conducted tours of Irish people, as well as a few acquaintances in England, France, and Italy, on the same route I twice traveled from coast to coast in the United States in 1967, visiting all the so-called trouble spots—New York, New Haven, Boston, Washington, Cleveland, Detroit, Chicago, Dallas, San Francisco, with a few side trips here and there in between.

My own belief is that the United States is going through a semibloodless revolution of immense proportions, a delayed continuation of the upsurging demand for human rights which was embodied in the revolution of 1775. Granted there are "sick" individuals in America, those who would deny to others what their own ancestors won for them in the New World. Granted there are assassinations, crimes of violence, riots, strikes, and student rebellions, arson and looting. But there are also millions of ordinary people who are determined that the millions of young, black, and poor will not be cheated out of their rightful heritage, who are ready to help them win it.

Two of the chief exponents of this dynamic, not "sick," philosophy, John and Robert Kennedy, have been brutally removed from the stage, but the show will go on. Others will take their place. As de Tocqueville observed over a century ago, each period of tumult and change in the history of mankind has resulted in ever-greater benefits for an ever-larger number of people. Nothing can stop this sometimes deflected or temporarily halted but never-ending, inevitable process.

The rewards accruing to the underprivileged in America have already been sizable. The status quo stoutly defended by William Buckley and his ilk would cause violent nervous indigestion among the Bourbons and Pharaohs of the past, not to mention those in charge of current Irish affairs. It is not an exaggeration to say that the average young *black* person in the United States today, boy or girl, is receiving a far better education than are the young people of Ireland. All one has to do is watch any of the current Irish TV quiz programs to get a fair idea of the colossal ignorance of the average person in Ireland, an ignorance which embraces the true grandeur of the country's history. After all, how can one expect the clergy, who are in charge of what is and isn't taught, to perpetuate the very deeds and thoughts they opposed tooth and nail at every stage in the past?

Specifically, one Sunday morning during my visit I turned on the television set in my New York hotel room and chanced on an hour's panel discussion engaged in by the civic leaders, black and white, of a Westchester County town, Larchmont or Mamaroneck, as I recall. The amount of educated thought applied to the problems of that single town during one hour exceeded the *total* educated thought that has been applied during the eight years I have been in Ireland against *all* the problems presently facing the Irish.

Occasionally a fairly spirited round-table discussion of some truly important subject—education, housing, old age, censorship—gets going on Irish TV. Inevitably within the following week there is a god-awful racket raised by the clergy and the politicians who complain bitterly that "unqualified" individuals shouldn't be allowed to air their views on something they know nothing about. They overlook the fact that the only way to "qualify" these people is to educate them. And one of the quickest ways to educate them is via these same round-table television discussions.

As Gladstone aptly observed when someone stated that the Irish weren't "ready" for home rule, the best way to prepare people for freedom is to set them free. It is a lesson not yet learned in Ireland. Television shows guilty of such unpardonable sins as open-ended discussions disappear at an alarming rate from the supposedly independent state-owned broadcasting system.

The essential element lacking in Irish thought and in Irish education today, which reached supreme heights of expression in the writings and speeches of Wolfe Tone, Jonathan Swift, and other Irish Protestants, which served as the flaming motivation of the Young Irish and ascended to a glorious climax in Padraic Pearse's proclamation of Irish independence, is the philosophy that the individual, acting on the basis of *personal* conscience, is in charge of his own destiny. The belief that discipline must be primarily *self*-imposed, not imposed by authority from above. That a society made up of such free individuals, each respecting the rights of others, can attain to heights undreamed of in an authoritarian society.

One can discover this philosophy as the primary element in classical Greek thought, as the underlying principle in the teachings of Christ, watch it slowly become submerged in imperial Rome, and then burst out again during the Renaissance. Johannes Erigena, noblest of all Irish intellects, anticipated the Renaissance by several centuries when he said in effect that authority based on force was no authority at all, and that pure reason had no need of authority to support it in a truly free society.

One can trace this philosophy in Western Europe from its majestic presentation in Shakespeare's writings, notably in *Julius Caesar*—"The fault, dear Brutus, is not in our stars,/But in ourselves, that we are underlings"—through such Continental giants as Voltaire, Rousseau, and Goethe, and in the United States from Jefferson and Franklin down to such twentieth-century champions of the people as Franklin Roosevelt and the brothers Kennedy. It set Pope John aside from Church leaders of the past few centuries and placed him in fundamental opposition to the entrenched Old Liners, the hard-bitten reactionaries who still hold a great deal of power in the Vatican.

It is this fundamental philosophy which, in spite of the torturous growing pains of living in a democracy, has caused most educated Westerners to turn their backs squarely against *both* communism and fascism, and which is causing so much trouble for totalitarian chieftains today in such countries as Poland, Yugoslavia, Rumania, Hungary, Czechoslovakia, as well as in Russia.

Specifically, it is what makes one writhe in anger at the continued presence of the Unionist/Orange Order dictatorship in Northern Ireland, working wittingly or unwittingly iron-hand-in-velvet-glove with the hierarchy, sly tongue not tucked in cheek, thwarting the deep-rooted if quiescent desire of some 78 percent of the total Irish people to be once more a united, indivisible nation.

Except for a few tolerated mavericks like Conor Cruise O'Brien and Séan MacBride, this concept of free individuals prospering in a free society is missing in modern Irish ecclesiastical and political circles.

The average "educated" Irish man or woman is oblivious to its very existence. And will continue to be while the Roman Catholic Church is calling the outmoded signals in the dear old Emerald Isle, God help us!

It is a great pity that the two countries most closely linked to Ireland by blood, as compared to bloodshed—France and the United States—play an infinitesimal role in the cultural, economic, and political development of the Irish nation. The ignorance and lack of understanding in France and America as to what is currently going on in Ireland is appalling. And the same thing is true of Irish knowledge and understanding of what is actually going on, and has gone on, in her two sister countries.

In the case of present-day Irish-Americans their immediate ancestors who crossed the Atlantic resolutely tried to forget the sorrows they had left behind and faced hopefully toward what lay ahead of them. They brought up their children and grandchildren oblivious to their three-thousand-year-old past except for a vague sentimentality. Most Irish-Americans who visit Ireland today either don't stay long enough to find out what's happening or are so overflowing with this same sentimentality that they are blind to reality. Austin Clarke put his finger on them in his poem, "Irish American Dignitary":

*Glanced down at Shannon from the sky-*
*way*
*With his attendant clergy, stayed night*
*In Dublin, but whole day with us*
*To find his father's cot, now dust*

*And rubble, bless new church, school*
*buildings*
*At Glantworth, drive to Spangle Hill*
*And cut first sod, hear, answer, fine*
*speeches*
*Accepted a learned gown, freedom*
*Of Ancient City, so many kissing*
*His ring—God love him!—almost*
*Missed the waiting liner: that day in Cork*
*Had scarcely time for knife and fork.*

As of now there is no effective program designed to create closer bonds between the United States and Ireland. Nor between Ireland and France. The Irish Export Board, with offices in New York and San Francisco, does a superb job helping Irish manufacturers sell to American, English, and French buyers, but while exports to the United States were increasing tenfold during the past decade, exports to the United Kingdom were increasing fifteenfold, so that the percentage of total exports to America is less now than it was in 1958.

Whereas the Jews in the United States, England, and elsewhere have contributed immeasurably to the development of Israel, the Irish government actively discourages any comparable help from overseas. It would appear that the hierarchy much prefers to leave "the Pope's policeman"—England—as represented today by trade and financial domination, the Protestant Ascendancy in the Republic, and the Unionist/Orange Lodge clique in the North, the primary foreign influence in Irish affairs.

When I was an early teen-ager in New Haven,

Connecticut, my family attended a ramshackle church covered with asphalt shingle near Beaver Pond Park, on the edge of what was then and still is a Negro ghetto. My father, who had recently escaped from the Irish ghetto on the other side of the New York, New Haven, and Hartford railroad tracks in Fair Haven, used to love to tell the story of two New England Roman Catholics; coming out of Notre Dame Cathedral in Paris, one of them turns to the other and says, "Well, Tom, this is one city where they can't say, 'I remember when we used to hunt rabbits out where the Catholic church now stands'." By the end of the 1920's the tar-papered edifice had been replaced by not one but two imposing fieldstone churches farther west in the city. It was a process repeated over and over again throughout America. Which wouldn't have happened if the Irish-Americans had taken the advice of their parish priests, had stayed on farms, and maintained the "traditional" Irish way of life.

Well, I can hear someone ask, "if you're so damned unhappy in Ireland, why don't you go back where you came from?"

But I *have* gone back where I came from. And I am living among those whom I look on as fellow countrymen. Nor am I unhappy. Far from it. As I trust is clear by now, my frustration stems from an overwhelming conviction that, *on the basis of what they have accomplished elsewhere in time and space,* the native Irish could be living far more fruitful, profound, and joyous lives than is now the case, could be creating one of the truly significant civilizations on this planet, rather than a second-class society. The very fact that Ireland is a paradise for those like myself who come from outside only throws into sharper relief the predicament of the home-grown Irish people. If I were a young native Irishman, North *or* South, I would leave the country within twenty-four hours and not come back unless and until I had prospered elsewhere.

After twenty-five years of working in New York, after living for long stretches in seven other countries, I can understand why Bernard Shaw said you had to see the rest of the world before you could fully appreciate Ireland. In Shaw's case it was love at second sight. He left Ireland in his early twenties, shedding no tears, and didn't return until he was past fifty.

In my case it was love at first sight. Strolling up Grafton Street from Trinity College to St. Stephen's Green a few hours after landing at Dublin Airport, unknowingly retracing for several hundred yards the route taken by Leopold Bloom on that memorable early June day, I felt at home as I had never felt before.

My reactions may have been partly psychological, but if I had had no blood ties with Ireland, I think I would have stayed anyway. By the time I had driven south through Wicklow and Waterford—for all the world like a great private park—had spent a few days in the little fishing hamlet of Ballycotton on the south coast, had wound my way through West Cork and Kerry, the oldest settled part of Ireland and still the most untouched, had savored for a few more days the thatched-roof charm of Adare in County Limerick, I knew I had found what I had been looking for.

Sometimes I wake up at night in winter with the wind whistling in across endless tracks of white-capped Atlantic Ocean, howling down the chimneys, and I say to myself, "What in the world are you doing here, you long-time habitué of the sidewalks of New York, you denizen of the skyscrapers? Have you lost your mind?" Then I summon up a thousand reasons why I am in Ireland and go right back to sleep.

If I were to visit Ireland for the first time, knowing what I know now, I would leave Dublin until last. Dublin is eighteenth and nineteenth century. Rural Ireland is ageless. I would get off at Shannon Airport in the west, head north, by back roads only, into Galway and across to Clonmacnoise—most fascinating of all Irish sites—then continue north by back roads into Donegal, returning south along the coast to Limerick City.

I would spend a week exploring the rivers and estuaries of County Limerick—Bunratty Castle, King John's slightly older stronghold on the Shannon by the Treaty Bridge in Limerick, the friaries, abbeys, churches, and castles at Askeaton, Adare, and Kilmallock, not overlooking nearby the haunted landscape of prehistoric Lough Gur. Next I would slowly circle the entire southern coast, not missing Valentia Island and St. Finan's Bay, the most exquisite panorama in all Ireland, on to Cork. From there I would cut inland to the mighty Rock of Cashel, wander in and out of several nearby ecclesiastical sites, including Jerpoint Abbey, then on through Clonmel and Kilkenny to the east coast.

By then one is ready for Dublin. By then you will be caught up by the lyric spirit of Ireland, the softly blended backdrop of landscape and climate, of woods and streams and fields and mountains that has formed all of her poets and playwrights, regardless of blood or heritage, into creative instruments whose expression, in spite of strong individuality, has been uniquely and distinctively Irish. By then you will understand why in their very essence the Irish are indestructible. Seemingly incapable of improving their lot. Yet at the same time indestructible.

Aside from the country itself, there are other blessings which make even more incomprehensible the present mediocre state of the Irish:

There is no huge defense budget, no heavy tax burden required to support such a budget. Nobody is mad at the Irish anymore. There is no menace of war, either sought by or thrust upon them. The guided missile or atom bomb that lands on Ireland will arrive through sheer accident.

Underpopulation—except for those forced to migrate each year—offers benefits to visitors and natives alike. There are no traffic snarls, except in a few sections of Dublin. In most rural areas one can drive for miles at any given time without meeting more than one or two cars. The impression grows that everybody is taking a siesta or has gone off to the races. There is no threat of famine, little pollution or squandering of natural resources.

Crimes of violence are almost nonexistent. Police officers go unarmed. Except for a few hardy perennials, prostitution has disappeared from Dublin along with Night Town, once among the largest and most depressing of waterfront red-light districts. There is no divorce problem, since divorce doesn't exist. No broken homes need be mended or patched together in new alliances.

Illegitimacy is still at a fairly high level, but foster parents are usually quietly provided through ecclesiastical channels. The Pill has slipped into Ireland, although unfortunately, as usually happens, it has been taken up by the upper rather than the low-income, large-family segment of the population.

The frightful poverty and squalor of fifty years ago has largely disappeared except in a handful of urban slum areas. Tuberculosis, once the scourge of the Irish, has been almost wiped out. Public drunkenness—inert bodies lying in ditches and stretched out along the highways, a common sight after race meetings and fairs thirty years ago—has ended. With a high percentage of adults total abstainers, it is impossible to work out any reliable per capita consumption figures, but acute alcoholism would seem to be no more of a problem than in most countries. During ten years I have not seen one person drunk on the streets.

There is no danger of sudden, violent political upheavals. Communism, except in the minds of a few old-line reactionaries, is no threat from within or without. There is no color problem. Unlike Holland, Portugal, Belgium, England, and France, no economic or social problems stemming from having had colonial possessions confront the Irish, an unexpected benefit for having formerly been themselves possessed.

The vital importance of the tourist trade pushes forward many a foot that would otherwise be dragging. Although the Irish Georgian Society on little money has done an outstanding job of preserving classical architecture and of attracting visitors to Ireland to see it, their task has been made easier, since more than one hard-bitten politician, who would like to see *all* buildings erected by the Ascendancy demolished, has restrained his hand because they are obviously "tourist attractions."

Similarly the many-sided Minister for Finance, Mr. Haughey, not only forced through in the face of much picayune opposition the widely acclaimed ROSC exhibition of world-famous painters in 1967, but has secured the funds for a greatly expanded long-term cultural program embracing the visual arts, music, ballet, and the theater. It is highly questionable whether this could have been done without the supporting argument, "it's good for the tourist trade." The same powerful lever has been applied in a number of similar situations.

Weighing these encouraging factors against the current overall situation, the question comes to mind, "What will Ireland be like after *another* fifty years?" It seems almost certain it will still be shuffling along in just about the same dreary fashion. "A great country to visit. Hardly a place in which to be born and raised." A terrible shame when one reflects on what sort of civilization the Irish are capable of building.

Most frustrating of all, *without losing any of the blessings they now enjoy,* it would take so little to release the Irish people from the straitjacket they are in:

*If* the Irish nation could be reunited, with Ireland forming a closer working relationship with England, Scotland, and Wales . . .

*If* the Irish Protestants could be brought back into the national mainstream and the specter of religious bitterness at long last laid to rest . . .

*If* the type of educational program envisioned by Donough O'Malley could be pushed through at all levels against any and all opposition . . .

*If* a broad, long-term social-welfare program, both North and South, covering housing, jobs,

> security for the old, could be launched and persisted in . . .
>
> *If* enlightened leaders would take over the ship of state from the hierarchy and set the nation on a fresh progressive course . . .
>
> *If* the clergy would offer the Irish people something more inspiring than the present "medieval" hocus pocus . . .

then, but not until then, will all things under heaven be possible. Until then Ireland will drift along the same dreary path, a third-rate republic full of first-class people.

In *John Bull's Other Island,* Bernard Shaw envisioned the society he hoped would evolve once the Irish nation was set free. Perhaps not by chance it is, as was the ancient Irish nation, threefold in nature:

> KEEGAN: In my dreams it is a country where the State is the Church and the Church the People: three in one and one in three. It is a commonwealth in which work is play and play is life: three in one and one in three. It is a temple in which the priest is the worshipper and the worshipper the worshipped: three in one and one in three. It is a godhead in which all life is human and all humanity is divine: three in one and one in three. It is, in short, the dream of a madman.

Today the Church, as never before, bestrides the Irish scene. The state, while overshadowed, is represented. Only the indestructible Irish people themselves, still being cheated out of their rightful heritage and ancient birthright, still being held down in the mire, have not yet emerged into the radiant sunlight. May the rebirth of their glory be not far off!

# INDEX